A Hole in Science

An Opening for an Alternative Understanding of Life

By Ted Christopher

ISBN 978-1-62967-069-0
Library of Congress Control Number 2016938757

*Dedicated to my old friends from
Laos and all other sincere people
with heretical views.*

Contents

Preface to the 2016 (2nd) Edition

A number of sentences in the original edition of this book were cleaned up some for this edition. Also some significant changes to portions of Chapter 6 and Chapter 7 were introduced. The book is still quite conceptual in a number of places - including Chapter 1 - and in combination with a somewhat terse writing style, that encourages slow reading.

Preface

The modern scientific understanding of life is built upon the belief that all features of life - including of course consciousness - are completely describable in terms of molecules and their activities. From this perspective, living beings can be viewed as simply constituting a particular subset of the material universe, and as such are presumably constrained by the same laws of physics and chemistry. This material-only hypothesis is usually referred to as scientific materialism or materialism, and it is essentially a modern intellectual fixture. The corresponding blueprints for organisms are of course believed to be given by a particular large molecule - deoxyribonucleic acid (DNA).

A couple of preliminary orientation notes. Hereafter the term "materialism" (or one of its synonyms) will only refer to the belief in the material-only nature of life (not the more general hypothesis about the universe). A second orientation note is that the focus herein will be primarily on humans, with secondary consideration given to other animals.

Now with regards to scientific materialism there are two basic points presented in this book. The first is that materialism has a big hole in it. This gap is centered on the unfolding "absolutely beyond belief" failure of DNA to determine some basic innate characteristics of individual humans and this possibility was apparent before the frustrating follow-up to the Human Genome Project. The second point is that this hole appears to be consistent with the common premodern transcendental understanding of life ("transcendental" will be used herein in place of a number of existing terms including "transmigration" and "reincarnation"). Starting with this preface I will lead with the first set of arguments and then follow up with some possible transcendental-based explanations. At a minimum I hope to get readers to see some serious challenges facing science's material-only vision, and also to encourage them to consider alternatives.

I get the ball rolling by taking a quote from Sam Harris' *Free Will* in which he pointed out that:

> And now your brain is making choices on the basis of preferences and beliefs that have been hammered into it over a lifetime - by your genes, your physical development since the moment you were conceived, and the interactions you had with other people, events, and ideas [Harris S. 2012, p.41].

Harris' message naturally flows from the materialist model. From that model's perspective, you are lucky to be alive given your dependence upon a very unlikely conception that produced your particular DNA blueprint, a blueprint that as Richard Dawkins put it, "created [you], body and mind" [Dawkins, p.20]. Continuing, that DNA blueprint (including the gene portions), defined your "nature" component and your subsequent environmental exposures formed your "nurture" component. From materialism's viewpoint that nurture dynamic was essentially updating or refining your innate programming. Thus, the material-only entity that is you; your particular behavior; and of course as a bio-robot, lack of free will. The particular molecules that constitute you just carry out their molecular activities and thus Harris can simply characterize you as a "biochemical puppet". Some of the potential significance of this materialist's perspective was made apparent in a June 2014 *Scientific American* article that pointed out some of the ways in which "skepticism about free will erodes ethical behavior" and how this could conceivably culminate in societal "anarchy" [Shariff and Vohs].

Now compare the previous quote with the following description of a musical prodigy found in Darold A. Treffert's *Islands of Genius*:

> By age five Jay had composed five symphonies. His fifth symphony, which was 190 pages and 1328 bars in

length, was professionally recorded by the London Symphony Orchestra for Sony Records. On a *60 Minutes* program in 2006 Jay's parents stated that Jay spontaneously began to draw little cellos on paper at age two. Neither parent was particularly musically inclined, and there were never any musical instruments, including a cello, in the home. At age three Jay asked if he could have a cello of his own. The parents took him to a music store and to their astonishment Jay picked up a miniature cello and began to play it. He had never seen a real cello before that day. After that he began to draw miniature cellos and placed them on music lines. That was the beginning of his composing.

Jay says that the music just streams into his head at lightning speed, sometimes several symphonies running simultaneously. "My unconscious directs my conscious mind at a mile a minute," he told the correspondent on that program [Treffert 2010, pp.55-56].

Treffert's book contains a number of other examples supporting his conclusion that prodigal (including prodigious savant) behavior typically involves "know[ing] things [that were] never learned". Such behaviors provide clear rebuts to the materialist vision and thus Harris' statement about free will. Treffert also considered the phenomenon of acquired savant syndrome in which savant behaviors appear in the wake of central nervous system setbacks. Needless to say, it is unlikely that puppets (or robots) would acquire skills as a result of physical damage.

An under-appreciated problem for the carved-in-scientific-stone, materialist vision is that there have always been counterexamples available in the form of unusual (and noncontroversial) behavioral phenomena. Additionally monozygotic twins - with shared DNA blueprints - are far too different. For example, take Harris' logic and then consider that with very similar environments and the same DNA, it turns out that if one monozygotic twin is gay then the likelihood that his twin brother will also be gay is only 20-30% (ironically found in Francis Collins' *The Language of Life: DNA and the Revolution in Personalized Medicine* [pp.204-205]). This is an example of the large differences found between monozygotic twins, differences which suggest a behavioral mystery potentially affecting all of us and which led Steven Pinker to acknowledge, "something is happening here but we don't know what it is" [Pinker 2002, p.380].

The big question, though, is how well can science in general confirm their Nature-plus-Nurture, material-only understanding of life? In September 2008, the geneticist David Goldstein (then at Duke University) was quoted regarding the outcome of thorough comparisons between the million or so common genetic (or DNA) variations and the apparent inheritance patterns associated with the occurrences of common complex diseases [Wade 2008]. It had naturally been assumed that some of these common variations amongst our DNA blueprints would be correlated with the patterns of susceptibility to common diseases (and of course to other innate differences between individuals). This assumption was also bolstered by estimates that very little DNA - perhaps 0.1% or about 3 million nucleotide elements - appears to differ between any two humans [Schafer; Green; Kingsley]. Somewhere then amongst this small subset of variable DNA there should be the origins of our innate differences, and this assumption is the basis of the fields and big expectations of personal genomics and behavioral genetics. But Goldstein pointed out that:

> [a]fter doing comprehensive studies for common diseases, we can explain only a few percent of the genetic component of most of these traits. For schizophrenia and bipolar disorder, we get almost nothing; for Type 2 diabetes, 20 variants, but they explain only 2 to 3 percent of familial clustering, and so on.

Goldstein then added:

It's an astounding thing that we have cracked open the human genome and can look at the entire complement of common genetic variants, and what do we find? Almost nothing. That is absolutely beyond belief.

Subsequently, in 2011 the director of the Bioscience Resource Project, Jonathan Latham, offered his own assessment:

The most likely explanation for why genes for common diseases have not been found is that, with few exceptions, they do not exist ... The likelihood that further searching might rescue the day appears slim. A much better use of the money would be to ask: if inherited genes are not to blame for our commonest illnesses, can we find out what it is [Latham]?

This surprising DNA deficit has been reflected not only in the lack of DNA breakthrough-headlines but also in the extraordinary failure of the associated biotechnology industry [Sheldrake, pp.168-171].

Nonetheless confident news may continue - such as with the junk DNA headlines of September 2012 - but significant findings with regards to our individual inheritances are still missing (the junk DNA news bonanza was later characterized by neurobiologist Athena Andreadis as a big "orchestrated PR campaign" [Andreadis]). Thus, in a 2012 blog contribution, geneticist Kevin A. Mitchell acknowledged that a "debate is raging in human genetics" over this missing heritability problem [Mitchell 2012/02]. This under-communicated scientific impasse offers a fundamental challenge to materialism, an understanding which might simply have been questioned based on some behavioral enigmas.

◆ ◆ ◆

The second argument in this book can be approached thru findings from studies of the natural religious or spiritual understanding of young children. In the book, *Born Believers - The Science of Children's Religious Belief*, Justin L. Barrett laid out some of the growing evidence that infants tend to possess an innate understanding of the existence of souls/God/gods, to be believers in what Barrett termed a "natural religion" [Barrett]. The book contained some striking examples including ones in which the positions of atheists' were rebutted by their young children. As Barrett wrote "[c]hildren are prone to believe in supernatural beings such as spirits, ghosts, angels, devils, and gods during the first four years of life" [p.3]. He later added:

> Exactly why believing in souls or spirits that survive death is so natural for children (and adults) is an area of active research and debate. A consensus has emerged that children are born believers in some kind of afterlife, but not why this is so [p.120].

These striking findings were simply placed within science's vision, though. Barrett, even as a practicing Christian, concluded that these are simply delusional tendencies derived from evolution and nurture - "biology plus ordinary environment". How our evolution-formed DNA blueprints could have resulted in such beliefs appears to be quite a mystery, though. At the beginning of his book Barrett did offer an alternative explanation that had been provided confidently by an Indian man he encountered on a train. In Barrett's words the man had explained:

> [T]hat on death, we go to be with God and are later reincarnated. As children had been with God more recently, they could understand God better than adults can. They had not yet forgotten or grown confused and distracted by the world. In a real sense, he explained, children came into this world knowing God more purely and accurately than adults do [p.2].

Some of the possible implications of that transcendental view will be explored herein, in particular in the context of the growing mystery of the origins of our innate individual specifics. This view appears to have been a common premodern understanding as described in *M'Clintock and Strong's Cyclopaedia of Biblical,*

Theological and Ecclesiastical Literature ,"[t]ransmigration, dating back to a remote antiquity, and being spread all over the world, seems to be anthropologically innate, and to be the first form in which the idea of immortality occurred to man" [Head and Cranston, p.170]. This belief has two aspects, the intuitive continuity of behavior/personality part and the much more puzzling cause-and-effect (or popularly "karma") part. Of these two logically distinct hypotheses it has been claimed that they were historically "in fact ... virtually always conjoined" [Head and Cranston, p.10]. Perhaps the apparent continuity of personalities across lives in small and undistracted populations initiated and then amplified the credibility of the continuity belief. Additionally, perhaps the karma hypothesis then followed on occasion from observing an individual encountering their apparent just deserts across lives. In a personal sense, a transcendental understanding would assert that at a core or foundational level, each of us is a non-material self or soul - a center of consciousness - which in the long run travels back and forth between embodied and disembodied existences (and thus transcends any particular one), and further that there is some continuity between these sequential existences.

In this book I will argue that in addition to offering a straightforward explanation for our natural religion, a transcendental perspective also provides traction on some scientific conundrums including prodigies, transgender individuals, and the surprising variations in personality found amongst a number of species; a simple explanation for the mysteries associated with monozygotic twins; a backdrop for some controversial phenomena including near-death experiences; and finally a consistent framework for the missing heritability problem. In brief, the missing origins for a number of our innate individual specifics could be understood as carryover from previous lives and with some standout behaviors - as with prodigious savants and prodigies - there could be some additional carryover consistent with some of the remarkable descriptions of the intervening disembodied state.

◆ ◆ ◆

This book serves the Religion-versus-Science debate by offering counterarguments to science's material-only, bio-robotic vision of life. In so doing it helps open a door to alternative understandings. In exploring some potential explanations provided by the premodern transcendental understanding I consider evidence for a transcendental soul and in so doing offer some bottom-up support for what I think is a religious perspective. On the other hand, the usual top-down approach of pursuing objective arguments for the existence of God is apparently very difficult. Furthermore, even if someone succeeded - perhaps with a physics-based effort like *The God Theory* [Haisch] or an evolution-required-some-intelligent-intervention effort like *Darwin's Doubt* [Meyer] - how would that ultimately change science's puppet-like vision of you and your life? A chapter taking a uniquely critical look at both religion and science is included.

The discussions in this book can also be seen as complementary to some of the established approaches to breaching scientific materialism. A sampling of these established efforts include investigations of extrasensory perception [Tart; Radin]; possible cases of reincarnation [Stevenson; Tucker 2005 and 2015]; near-death experiences [Holden et al; Alexander]; the totality of psychological challenges as chronicled in a thorough text like *Irreducible Mind* [Kelly et al]; and also more broadly-based challenges to materialism [Sheldrake]. This book on the other hand, focuses on materialism's inheritance problem along with some consistent explanations available with the common premodern transcendental understanding. Some possible reincarnation cases will be used herein, though, as they offer some support for general transcendental hypotheses.

The perplexing range of personalities found among people and other species; the surprising differences found between identical twins; and also our innate religious inclinations; all challenge scientific materialism. Together with some behavioral conundrums and the unfolding "beyond belief" missing heritability problem, it is time to question the completeness of biology's view of life. In *The*

Sacred Depths of Nature, this view was confidently characterized by the author/biologist Ursula Goodenough, as "relentlessly mechanical", "bluntly deterministic", and by extension without free will [Goodenough, pp.46-47]. As will be shown herein, though, contradictions to this view are easy to find.

Chapter 1

The Quietly Unfolding
Missing Heritability Problem

Arguably the ground floor of the modern intellectual point of view is science's material-only understanding of life. With the possible exception of those making inferences drawn from near-death experiences or parapsychological studies, the modern mechanistic paradigm enjoys thorough intellectual confidence. It would be a challenge to try to identify academic efforts in the last 50 years that have questioned this ground floor of science's vision, perhaps in particular that our deoxyribonucleic acid (DNA) "created us, body and mind" and therefore that our individual existences came against gargantuan odds. This view of DNA is made explicit in the title of Francis S. Collins' 2010 book about DNA, *The Language of Life*. This vision of life is of course nested within the modern scientific vision of the universe - vast and meaningless.

Some DNA Basics

Before considering some recent efforts to identify the DNA origins of particular characteristics of individuals, it is worth considering some relevant aspects of the DNA landscape. I start here with a somewhat detailed example to warm up to some evolutionary dynamics of DNA and their constituent genes. A relatively concrete and significant example of those dynamics was the development of color vision in our primate ancestors. As a result of that development humans and a number of other primate species differ from most mammalian species in our increased capacity to distinguish the visual spectrum. In particular, our eyes' retinas come equipped with three distinct visual pigments, one of which responds strongest to short-wavelengths of light and the other two respond strongest to longer wavelengths. Those responses of the three pigments correspond to the colors blue, green, and red, respectively. With their differing spectral sensitivities, these pigments together provide the necessary input so that our brains can provide relatively good color vision. Details of how the brain's basic visual processing occurs are still being worked out, but the evolutionary development and significance of our trichromatic vision (or trichromacy) appears to be understood. The relevant source here - a fine *Scientific American* article, "The Evolution of Primate Color Vision", by Gerald H. Jacobs and Jeremy Nathans - included a revealing picture of a frog as our trichromatic vision would see it and another from the corresponding typical mammalian dichromatic viewpoint [Jacobs and Nathan]. The article also pointed out that a consequence of our trichromatism "is that computer and television displays can mix red, green, and blue pixels to generate what we perceive as a full spectrum of color".

A pigment consists of a light-absorbing molecule derived from vitamin A together with a protein bearing a particular sensitivity to optical or light stimulation. Such pigments when housed in one of our retinas' cone cells can be stimulated by some light and that response is then relayed to the brain for producing an image. The specification for a visual pigment's protein is found in the DNA. It appears that the DNA specification for our shorter-wavelength pigment protein is essentially shared with many other vertebrates. Thus it appears that this DNA protein-specification (or gene) apparently had its origins a long time ago in evolutionary history.

It is with the DNA specifications for our two long-wavelength pigment proteins that some interesting history and the specific origins of our color vision can be found. These two genes - and the resulting pigment proteins - are very similar, and in fact, the two proteins differ in only 3 out of their constituent 364 amino acid elements. Many other vertebrates also have a single visual pigment similar to these but somehow in evolutionary history one or more primates got an update, an almost-duplication, resulting in a second long-wavelength pigment specification and with it an opportunity for improved color vision.

The initial step towards our trichromacy appears to have occurred over 40 million years ago in some primate ancestors and involved successive changes or mutations in the original long-wavelength pigment gene. These mutations left these primate ancestors with three variations (or alleles) amongst their long-wavelength gene which was located on their X chromosomes. Since there was only one such specification per X chromosome, though, the males in this group (having only one X chromosome) were still limited to two color-sensitive retinal pigments and thus some form of dichromatic vision. Some of the females, on the other hand, were fortunate in that their two X chromosomes bore different long-wavelength pigment genes and thus they experienced trichromacy. This original gender-dependent step towards trichromacy is still present in the New World primates of South and Central America.

After the separation of the New and Old World primates (via the moving apart of South America and Africa) about 40 million years ago, there appears to have been a rare error in the production of a subsequently fertilized egg cell within the Old World primate lineage of Africa and Asia. That error apparently occurred in the chromosome-swapping (or recombination) process used to form an egg cell and occurred in a female with DNA that bore two different long-wavelength pigment genes. The particular error apparently left two distinct long-wavelength genes on one X chromosome. Thus, that resulting egg cell's DNA became a ticket for its offspring to possess trichromatic vision regardless of their gender.

The resulting vision update was likely helpful to those primates including with their efforts to distinguish ripe fruit. Over subsequent generations then this dual long wavelength gene package spread widely to provide the trichromatic vision that is now standard equipment amongst Old World primates including humans. The original arrangement with only one longer-wavelength pigment gene on the X chromosome would have fared poorly under natural selection, and thus was eventually lost from the Old World primates' gene pool.

The evolutionary dynamic exhibited by this development of trichromatic vision in Old World primates was perhaps somewhat complicated with its sequence of mutations followed by a recombination error. But the underlying changes over time in DNA blueprints and then the subsequent response of natural selection - in this case positive selection - was not unusual. Thus as is currently understood, by happenstance a gender-independent trichromatic DNA specification was come upon long ago in the Old World primate lineage and it was a natural selection-winner so that over subsequent generations that trichromatic specification became the norm. (A subtle point being glossed over here is that the mammalian brain - as demonstrated in experiments with mice - apparently can readily incorporate the additional input of a second long-wavelength visual pigment and thus utilize a trichromatic opportunity).

What is of general note here is the very elemental, undirected, and long term nature of the color vision evolutionary process. Another example of such a process can be found with the receptors responsible for our sense of smell which were cumulatively built over time and involved about a thousand genes. Each of those genes was acquired during evolutionary history and each produces a distinct protein which is used as chemical receptor in our nose and then also as a guide to ensure that the corresponding neural connection is correctly made in our brain [Pinker 2002, p.93]. Like the addition of the third visual pigment gene, the additions of each of these smell receptor genes was likely helpful in a reproduction-and-survival sense (perhaps in helping to distinguish a threat), and thus spread widely.

One additional complication associated with the genetics of our color vision, though, is that it is imperfect. Most significantly, there is some evolution-given variation in the two long wavelength genes found within the human genome. As a result of that variation about 1 in 12 males of European ancestry suffers from some form of deficiency in their ability to distinguish within the red-to-green light spectrum. Because these genes are located on the X chromosome, females are less likely to experience this condition and for the corresponding female population the deficiency figure is only about 1 in 200 [Columbia, p.626]. For other groups the occurrence rates appear to be lower. This second genetic dimension, involving DNA defining the differences between individuals within a species is of course important in and of itself, and is also fundamental to the ideas considered within this book.

Some other examples of DNA's confirmed individual import were given in David M. Kingsley's *Scientific American* article, "From Atoms to Traits" [Kingsley]. Kingsley pointed out several physical traits and their confirmed DNA origins. Sometimes these origins simply involve single element (or letter) changes in the DNA as in the case of short-versus-tall pea plants. In another example it entailed a big singular change involving the substitution of an 800-base-pair sequence into a gene of a pea plant resulting in wrinkled pea skins in place of smooth ones. The effects of these DNA variations had been noted by Gregor Mendel in the mid-nineteenth century. Along these lines Kingsley also pointed out that:

> bigger muscles, faster running ability or improved ability to digest new foods have all arisen from simple new arrangements of atoms in the DNA sequence of ... dogs and humans.

Amongst physical traits the DNA connection is increasingly being confirmed.

But it is also worth noting, though, that how an elemental DNA dynamic - like that found in our color vision history - could have formed something like complex instinctive behavioral tendencies is not easy to see. As Rupert Sheldrake pointed out:

> [g]enes are not selfish and ruthless, as if they contained gangster homunculi. Nor are they plans or instructions

for organisms. They merely code for the sequences of amino acids in protein molecules [Sheldrake, p.163].

Nonetheless, a number of species exhibit an unlearned or instinctive fear of snakes and it is a challenge to imagine discrete changes in the DNA code resulting in an automatic ability to become alarmed over the sight of a snake. Strongly detecting a particular frequency of light is a bit of a one-dimensional challenge for evolution, but detecting the visual form of particular objects is much more difficult. As non-infants most of us effortlessly see a visual field full of particular objects (including trees, dogs, roads, garbage cans, and clouds), and that process is built upon our past efforts to learn the appearances of those objects.

Continuing with a behavioral commentary, the particular context for humanity's mostly-mental evolutionary trek was nicely framed by Steven Pinker when he wrote:

> [o]ur minds are adapted to the small foraging bands in which our family spent ninety-nine percent of its existence, not the topsy-turvy contingencies we created since the agricultural and industrial revolutions [Pinker 1997, p.207].

Further, he characterized the corresponding environmental selection pressure as "a camping trip that never end[ed]" [Pinker 1997, p.207] Very little about this evolutionary scenario, though, appears to suggests that there could be genes - or more generally DNA - making substantial contributions to complex modern behaviors like playing the piano, being a Democrat, being adept to the demands of the Industrial Revolution, or being a natural whiz at calendar calculations. Thus, the associated DNA-based logic of behavioral genetics would appear to be a challenge for the underlying elemental nature of evolution. Nonetheless, science has puts its faith in the individual-defining import of DNA. As a frank testament to this faith, Steven Pinker confidently pointed out that:

> [i]dentical twins separated at birth [with maximal DNA similarity and gross environmental differences] share

traits like entering the water backwards and only up to their knees, sitting out elections because they feel insufficiently informed, obsessively counting everything in sight, becoming captain of the volunteer fire department, and leaving little love notes around the house for their wives [Pinker 1997, p.20].

Such optimism about DNA's behavioral impact appears to be commonly assumed and thus the cliche "it's in the DNA".

Another optimistic assessment was made by an editor of *Nature* who proclaimed that in the coming century:

[g]enomics will allow us to alter entire organisms out of recognition, to suit our tastes ... [and] will allow us to fashion the human form into any conceivable shape. We will have extra limbs, if we want them, and maybe even wings to fly [Nature 1997].

Putting aside such opinions, a number of basic assumptions about DNA's role are being tested thoroughly as (existing) DNA specifications are being compared against the corresponding individual outcomes.

◆ ◆ ◆

A return to one of the Preface's quotes by Duke University's geneticist David Goldstein is good place to embark on an overview of the missing DNA situation. In that September 2008 *New York Times* article Goldstein was quoted on the outcome of thorough efforts to try to identify the commonly occurring genetic variations (or common variants) which were presumed to contribute to the inheritance patterns found amongst the occurrences of common complex diseases like diabetes, cancer, heart disease, and mental illnesses [Wade 2008]. Part of the logic of this effort is reflected in the routine medical practice of asking patients about possible family histories of complex diseases since such diseases do tend to run in families. On the DNA side, the particular variations considered were single letter or nucleotide sites that commonly differ amongst individuals and also tend to coexist with larger variations at nearby gene portions of the DNA. These single nucleotide variations are called SNPs ("P" is for polymorphisms) and they tend to flag potentially significant changes in a nearby genes. But after thorough studies Goldstein concluded that:

> It's an astounding thing that we have cracked open the human genome and can look at the entire complement of common genetic variants, and what do we find? Almost nothing. That is absolutely beyond belief.

This was a rare frank assessment of the failure of the initial big scientific push to establish the "miracle" of personalized medicine via identifying the underlying DNA variations believed to be responsible for the common complex disease susceptibilities.

In October 2010 came another sober report from the personalized medicine front in an article in *Scientific American* entitled "Revolution Postponed" by Stephen S. Hall [Hall]. By this time Goldstein had some company in his negative assessment of the common variants hypothesis ("common" usually implies that a particular DNA code variation is present in at least 5 percent of humans), although the lack of positive connections notwithstanding, there were other geneticists still confident in the original hypothesis. The article touched on the significant rift existing between the two camps of geneticists. The alternative approach of others including Goldstein was then to pursue the complementary rare variants hypothesis and with it to assume that in a relatively short evolutionary period that natural selection had successfully weeded out the unhealthy common DNA variations present in the human gene pool. Commonly occurring disease-prone designs were thus assumed by this rare variants camp to have been consistent natural selection failures and thus lost in our reproductive history.

Amongst those resigned to the failure of the original common variants hypothesis, was Walter Bodner "who was among the first to propose the genome project in the 1980's and is a pioneer of the association studies that have dominated recent genomics". Bodner claimed that "[t]he vast majority of [these common] variants have shed no light on the biology of diseases" and also that the associated search was "scientifically wrong". David Botstein of Princeton University called the underlying search for SNPs (specifically the HapMap project) a "magnificent failure." And in the summer of 2010 Goldstein had said of the common variants hypothesis, "[w]e have entered and left that field, which explained less than a lot of people thought it would."

In the "Revolution Postponed" article the remaining supporters of the common variant hypothesis mentioned included Eric S. Lander of the Broad Institute at M.I.T. Lander claimed that over the previous three years findings into the genetic origins of diseases had been "mind blowing" and further that "we haven't even scratched the surface of common variants yet." His take was that the common variants hypothesis would eventually pan out. Another prominent supporter cited in Hall's article was Francis Collins, head of the National Institute of Health, who had claimed on an appearance on PBS's *The Charlie Rose Show* that via some new common variants findings "we have ... already ... change[d] our entire view of how to develop new therapeutics for diabetes, for cancer, for heart disease".

The gist conveyed in Hall's article, though, was of very limited success up to that time from the common variant-based genome studies. One enumerated example given was for type 2 diabetes. According to David Goldstein for this condition the:

> association studies analyzing 2.2 million SNPs in more than 10,000 people have identified 18 SNPs associated with the disease, yet these sites in total explain only 6 percent of the heritability of the disease - and almost none of the causal biology.

The closing reference to causal biology is a practical point since understanding this is viewed as essential to developing medical treatments to combat the disease susceptibilities. With the above numbers one might wonder about the statistical creditability of finding a 6 percent contribution distributed amongst 18 contributors (from amidst 2.2 million possible contributors). Those are pretty thin slices of the heritability pie and thus perhaps the worries of some researchers that these thin slices were really statistical illusions [Wade 2010].

Perhaps due to the solid logic behind it and also substantial investigative momentum, the common variants hypothesis subsequently extended itself into a search for "a large number of small-effect common variants" [Gibson]. The idea here was to try to find genetic causation through the sum of many small common variant contributions. Given the lack of significant findings reported in the subsequent years, though, it appears that neither of the common or rare variant camps (or variations thereof) has found much. And thus as mentioned earlier, a 2012 blog contribution by a neurogeneticist from Trinity College Dublin, Dr. Kevin A. Mitchell, acknowledged that:

> [a] debate is raging in human genetics these days as to why the massive genome-wide association studies [GWAs] that have been carried out for every trait and disorder imaginable over the last several years have not explained more of the underlying heritability [Mitchell 2012/02].

◆ ◆ ◆

Now stepping back from the DNA heritability search front, it is worth considering some more of the DNA landscape. In a May 2009 *Scientific American* article by Katherine S. Pollard entitled "What Makes Us Human?" the initial findings of efforts to determine the DNA differences underlying the species divide between humans and chimpanzees was presented [Pollard]. Pollard pointed out:

> [a] humbling truth emerged: our DNA blueprints are nearly 99 percent identical to theirs. That is, of the three billion letters that make up the human genome, only 15 million of them - less than 1 percent - have

changed in the six million years of so since the human and chimp lineages diverged.

Pollard then went on to point that:

> [e]volutionary theory holds that the vast majority of these changes had little or no effect on our biology. But somewhere among those roughly 15 million bases lay the differences that made us human.

An additional point could well have been made here and it is that somewhere amongst this inter-species defining collection of DNA letters (or nucleotides) there should also be a subset that is very relevant to the differentiating of our individual inheritances. This would seem to be particularly true for mental inheritances since our large brains are our big evolutionary distinction and as such were central to Pollard's article.

The above point about evolutionary theory is also significant to the basics of the dynamics of DNA. That theory asserts that the process of genomic change is in large part a haphazard one, as one evolutionary biologist, T. Ryan Gregory of Ontario's University of Guelph, stated, "[a]t its most fundamental level, it's a mess". This quote was given in an aptly entitled *New York Times Magazine* article, "Is Most of Our DNA Garbage?" [Zimmer 2015]. Thus in addition to functional dynamics similar to the previous ones dealing with vision and smell, there are also plenty of minimally functional dynamics too. Thus in a gross sense you can find relatively simple species like an onion or a broad-footed salamander with genomes far larger than those of humans - five and fifty times larger, respectively. From this perspective it appears that much of any species' genome - including ours - is simply "junk" or noncoding letter sequences that just happened to have hitched a ride on the DNA. It also appears that in some cases junk code segments had previously lost their functional or coding status via mutations during evolutionary history but nonetheless stayed on board the DNA. In a bottom line quote, the evolutionary biologist Gregory could assert that only "8 percent, plus or minus 1 percent" of the human genome is likely to be functional, and that the remainder, "doesn't seem to matter that much".

Finally, on the most relevant point from the DNA landscape, it turns out that Homo sapiens have been referred to by geneticists as a "small species" since there is relatively little genetic variation amongst us, and such limited variation is typical of a species with a small population [Pinker 2002, p.142-143]. That lack of genetic variation apparently followed from our having literally been a small species not too long ago as we survived through a period in which our population became tiny. An insufficient amount of time - evolution-wise - has since elapsed for that limited pool of DNA variation to expand much (unlike our population). Thus again, some estimates have it that any two human beings are about 99.9% identical in terms of their DNA blueprints, which translates to being different in about 3 million bases or letters [Schafer, Green, Kingsley]. It is also worth noting that even amongst this 0.1% variable portion of our genomes, there could be plenty of irrelevant junk. Thus, amongst the often cited three billion nucleotides figure there would seem to be a pretty small subset of our DNA, in particular amongst the variable portion, that should be home to our missing heritability. This was likely relevant to Goldstein's "absolutely beyond belief" characterization in 2008 of the initial failure of the common variants hypothesis.

◆ ◆ ◆

Now moving on for a focused behavioral look at the state of the heritability situation, it is worth considering the search for the origins of the variation in human intelligence. An October 2008 *Scientific American* article "The Search for Intelligence" offered this, as well as providing some context for intelligence which is arguably the biggest item on the behavioral genetics queue [Zimmer 2008]. The common variants hypothesis had again not panned out as it only appeared to offer a possible 0.4 percent explanation for the heritable - and thus presumed genetic - differences found amongst the intelligence scores considered. The article included University of Virginia psychologist Erik Turkheimer bolstering our intuitions in pointing out that intelligence "[i]s something that everybody observes in others" (unlike disease susceptibilities) and further that "intelligence and intelligence test scores are in many ways the best predictor in all of psychology". Intelligence, or perhaps more specifically academic intelligence, is certainly a big deal in modern societies. In the article it was pointed out that there appear to be neural (or brain) correlates associated with the variations in intelligence. Thus, perhaps in the future there could be a brain-imaging alternative to IQ tests. These could offer visual evidence letting you know how smart you are or should be and, in so doing, sidestep complications with regards to test-taking vagaries.

Moving on four years and that search received an update in an article by David Dobbs in which he reported on findings that had apparently more than doubled the DNA origins identified to 1 percent [Dobbs]. Some might argue against the ultimate significance (or survivability) of that 1 percent but even an insider like psychologist Robert Plomin of King's College London sounded resigned to the situation, "[i]f it's this hard to find an effect of just 1 percent what you're really showing is that the cup is 99 percent empty". Needless to say this is very surprising conclusion from the scientific perspective.

The same Dobbs article described a theory accounting for the apparent lack of a DNA basis for the variation in the innate portion of IQ. The geneticist Dr. Kevin Mitchell, had proposed in a July 2012 blog effort that we should consider flipping the intelligence heritability logic around [Mitchell 2012/07]. Instead of looking at the genetics of intelligence we might consider high intelligence as the standard genetic equipment and consider the reverse genetic dynamic of dumbing instead - in particular dumbing via random genetic (or DNA) mutations. In this theory high functioning intelligence was a big evolutionary winner (perhaps akin to color vision amongst primates) and thus as offsprings of that process the DNA code responsible for high intelligence is found in most if not all of us. Then to cover the substantial variation in our innate intellectual capacities, Mitchell suggested we consider that random mutations - the numbers of which do vary amongst individuals (with an average of perhaps 100 mutations) - are the dynamic factor in the intelligence realm. This dumbing hypothesis is built upon the basic assumption that the impact of a DNA mutation is much more likely to be harmful than helpful. Random mutations do seem unlikely to beget high intelligence.

As suggested in Dobbs' article, Mitchell's theory of the dumbing down of intelligence appeared to have some traction amongst geneticists. Given the circumstances - little if any regular DNA support for such a big variable and largely innate behavioral attribute - it is not clear what alternatives were scientifically plausible. But stepping back, how much sense does this theory really make? When reading evolutionary psychology pieces, they tend to make both evolutionary sense and also immediate personal sense. For example a number of the various sexual behavioral theories are backed by clear evolutionary logic. The purported behavioral tendencies likely would have been advantageous to our ancestor's reproduction efforts and thus any underlying responsible genes would have spread widely. And in an intimate sense one can readily observe in oneself and others some of these behavioral tendencies. But does Einstein's intellect seem plausible as an evolutionary outcome? This topic and some relevant intelligence-related conundrums will be returned to in the following chapter.

◆ ◆ ◆

In another behavioral domain, the earlier David Goldstein quote pointed out that the search for common genetic variations had uncovered "almost nothing" in the way of connections to the occurrences of bipolar disorder and schizophrenia. An update on the schizophrenia genetic search can be gleaned from an article by Stanford University's Tanya Marie Luhrmann in the Summer 2012 issue of the *Wilson Quarterly* [Luhrmann]. In that "Beyond the Brain" article Luhrmann chronicled the general failure of the treatment of mental illness via what is referred to as the "bio-bio-

bio model". That biology-oriented approach had focused on such illnesses as expressions of a "brain lesion, [with a] genetic cause, and [an associated] pharmacological cure". This has not worked well thus far and in particular the underlying "search for a genetic explanation fell apart". Luhrmann described that:

> [t]he number of implicated genes is so great that Schizophrenia Forum, an excellent Web site devoted to organizing the scientific research on the disorder - the subject of 50,000 published articles in the last two decades - features what [one leading researcher Ridha] Joober has called a "gene of the week" section. Another [prominent researcher], Robin Murray ... has pointed out that you can now track the scientific status of a gene the way you follow the performance of a sports team.

These investigators apparently were finding no significant DNA basis for the inheritance of the susceptibility to schizophrenia, but the enormous momentum of the process had them chasing down statistical noise. This could well be happening elsewhere as expressions of the missing heritability problem.

A good deal of Luhrmann's article resonated with a message in Ethan Watter's critical look at mental illness in the modern world, *Crazy Like Us: The Globalization of the American Psyche*. Essentially the scientific assumptions - in particular the underlying materialist model with its presumed genetic origins - may be accurate but the implementation has thus far not worked. Traditional approaches to episodes of schizophrenia seem to have worked better than those of modern medical science. As Luhrmann pointed out, "[s]chizophrenia has a more benign course and outcome in the developing world". She also touched on the underlying downside of science's bio-robotic perspective (a perspective captured in the title, "Faulty Circuits", of an April 2010 *Scientific American* article by the director of the National Institute of Mental Health, Thomas Insel). In our country people with schizophrenia commonly spend a lot of time homeless in part because "[t]hey dislike the diagnosis even more than the idea of being out on the street, because for them the idea of being 'crazy'" is worse. Luhrmann also wrote that "Indian families don't treat people with schizophrenia as if they have a soul-destroying illness."

Identical Twins

One intuitive vantage point from which to see a number of the difficulties confronting the DNA model - and also the encompassing materialist vision - is with monozygotic twins. These so called identical twins in fact present a number of basic mysteries. The cause of their origin - the initial split or division of a single cell zygote - is a mystery. So is its occurrence only in some species. Further, similar appearances and biological-presumptions aside, the empirical realities of the resulting twins constitute a significant challenge to the sacred DNA "created us body and mind" logic that motivated the Human Genome efforts and associated excitement.

Although DNA replicas, such twins whether they were raised together or separately, have been observed on average to be more different than alike personality-wise. Thus these clones can closely share the same environment or inhabit separate ones (with whatever differences in epigenetic implications) and still they appear to have comparably different personalities. Notice this environment (or nurture) minimizing finding is also consistent with the conclusions of adoption studies. With some personal exposure to identical twins and/or after reading relevant study data, it should not come as a surprise that one conjoined (attached) monozygotic twin commented that "[w]e are two completely separate individuals who are stuck to each other. We have different world views, we have different lifestyles, we think very differently about issues" [Harris J., p.1]. This mystery motivated Judith R. Harris' *No Two Alike* and was discussed at some length in Steven Pinker's *The Blank Slate* [Pinker 2002].

Yet in the case in which identical twins were separated at birth, they can still share remarkably specific behavioral tendencies as mentioned in an earlier quote from Pinker. From the small and questionable stuff (look enough and any pair of humans might find they share some little preferences) to the big and life-defining stuff - like becoming very dedicated volunteer firemen [Segal, p.14]. Such phenomena have been used as strong evidence for the life-defining import of DNA, but set against the seemingly innate personality differences they could be just another mystery.

Large health differences between monozygotic twins were described in a 2006 *New York Times* article by Gina Kolata [Kolata 2006]. That article opened by describing a healthy and active 92 year old and her identical twin. The latter "is incontinent, she has had a hip replacement, and she has a degenerative disorder that destroyed most of her vision ... [and] has dementia". Yet the sisters have the same DNA, grew up together, and lived in the same place. They also had markedly different personalities and ambitions.

The centerpiece of Kolata's article was a description of a large study comparing the variations in longevities found amongst identical and same-sex fraternal (or dizygotic) twins. Since the former share all of their variable (and potentially individual-differentiating) DNA and the latter only half, comparisons like this are standard practice for determining the relative import of DNA, as in behavioral genetics. Continuing, together the study's twin populations totaled 10,251 pairs. The study found that the identical twins died only a little closer together than the fraternal twins and, specifically, the deaths of the identical twins averaged "more than 10 years apart". Consistent with this, one of the twin study's authors commented "[h]ow tall your parents are compared to the average height explains 80 to 90 percent of how tall you are compared to the average person [but] only 3 percent of how long you live compared to the average person can be explained by how long your parents lived". The relevant *Nature Review Genetics* paper gave the inferred genetic component as covering - "about a quarter of the variance in adult lifespan" - and pointed out that somewhat surprisingly, "the genetic influences on lifespan are minimal before the age of 60 and only increase after that age" [Christensen et al]. As representative of the intellectual momentum associated with

DNA (and science), though, Kolata's article had been titled "Live Long? Die Young? Answer Isn't Just Found in Genes".

Kolata's article also mentioned that "randomness" had been found amongst the longevity of genetically identical lab animals. Additionally, Dr. Robert Hoover of the National Cancer Institute was quoted from an editorial on the cancer connection, "there is a low absolute probability that a cancer will develop in a person whose identical twin - a person with an identical genome and many similar exposures - has the same type of cancer."

It is noteworthy, though, that these very significant and unexpected findings (and article) seem to have been minimally integrated into relevant scientific communication. This is possibly common for results that challenge materialism. For example, four years later in a *Scientific American* review article on the lack of findings in personal genomics the word "twin" never appeared [Hall]. If you are trying to find DNA which is significant to the different health outcomes of individuals who are broadly separated by environment and their variable portions of DNA, wouldn't it be good idea to gauge these efforts - and more generally inform others - on the large health differences found between individuals who are minimally separated by environment and share their DNA specifications?

Another monozygotic conundrum is the remarkable bond that tends to exist between them. As pointed out by Steven Pinker, "when separated at birth and reunited as adults, ... say they feel like they have known each other all their lives" [Pinker 2002, p.47]. In one of my childhood neighborhoods I can't even remember the local twins being apart. Given that siblicide is common in nature does this really make sense for siblings [Tenneson]?

Finally, another monozygotic-mystery can be found with regards to male exclusive homosexuality. This behavioral tendency appears to be established by birth and of course is a challenge to evolutionary reasoning. The DNA contributions can not be big, though, since when one monozygotic twin is gay then the other twin is gay in only about 20 to 30 percent of cases (against a backdrop overall gay frequency of 2 to 4 percent). Additionally, it appears that the likelihood of a male having a homosexual orientation increases by about 30 percent for each older brother preceding him. As mentioned earlier this information was found in Francis S. Collins' confident DNA book, *The Language of Life* [Collins, pp.204-205]. Thus science's gay explanation has to identify a loose DNA contribution, find the means to ramp up the gay likelihood by 30 percent per older brother (presumed to be caused by the mother's previous male-pregnancy experiences), and also perhaps identify some other subtle prenatal environmental influences to wedge apart the twins' orientations. Does this seem "bluntly deterministic" or consistent with the earlier cited programmatic assessment of Sam Harris? In fact these findings, like others not related to appearance, are contrary to DNA-based expectations and suggestive of a broadly-based mystery.

Transcendental Introduction

I switch gears here now to introduce a possible transcendental take on the DNA impasse as well as some neighboring mysteries. This alternative take is based on the common premodern transcendental understanding of life in which there is also an underlying soul reincarnating from life-to-life, and this non-material aspect can have far-reaching effects. On the prevalence as given previously from *M'Clintock and Strong's Cyclopaedia of Biblical, Theological and Ecclesiastical Literature*, "[t]ransmigration ... being spread all over the world, seems to be anthropologically innate" [Head and Cranston, p.170]. This belief has two components, the relatively intuitive behavioral continuity aspect and the very puzzling cause-and-effect (or popularly "karma") aspect. As mentioned earlier, these two distinct hypotheses were claimed to have been historically packaged together [Head and Cranston, p.10]. Perhaps within small isolated groups the appearance of the continuity of personality and interests across lives helped to establish the continuity hypothesis. Also the karma hypothesis might have followed from instances in which individuals exhibiting such continuity also appeared to experience consequences consistent with the previous individual's (or incarnation's) efforts.

A transcendental continuity understanding would be consistent with individual cases suggestive of young children experiencing an explicit recall of a previous life [Stevenson; Tucker; Leininger] and also with our innate dualism. The continuity aspect also offers explanations for a number of surprising behaviors including those found amongst prodigies, transgender individuals and adoptees. Further it could provide insight into the very surprising personalities found amongst a number of species [Siebert, Angier 2010]. Continuity also offers a simple explanation for the behavioral differences found between monozygotic twins and more generally a consistent framework for the behavioral side of the missing heritability problem. With the second - the cause-and-effect - transcendental component, there appears to be consistency with the unexpectedly large health differences found between monozygotic twins and moreover with the disease susceptibility portion of the missing heritability problem. Thus, the missing DNA origins for a number of individual characteristics could be viewed as expressions of carryover from previous lives and with some exceptional behaviors - as with prodigies and prodigious savants - there could be some additional carryover consistent with some premodern descriptions of the disembodied state.

A further suggested generalization is that transcendental import would likely be overlapping with, as well as complementary to, the import of DNA. If, as some traditions assert, the incarnating soul is drawn to their parents-to-be, then that soul might tend to find some continuity in the DNA specifics produced by conception - beyond the species and sex default codes. This could include DNA-determined unusual conditions. But beyond this overlapping aspect, though, the odds that the crapshoot of conception would deliver a variable DNA match for a soul's overall trajectory is zero. The DNA definition would have to be breached in many ways. Thus to the degree that science can show that DNA plus realistic environmental impacts define individuals, then this would minimize the import associated with possible transcendental phenomena. In this regard, efforts to confirm the DNA expectations of behavioral genetics and also to account for the surprising differences found between monozygotic twins are of particular interest.

A complication being glossed over here is that in a number of cases the DNA blueprint's import is hypothesized by science to be probabilistic and thus the relevant confirmation here would have to be carried out as an averaging-exercise over many individuals. For example, from this perspective there should be one or more DNA codes specifying for the tendency to be a transgender individual and thus individuals bearing such a code should be more likely to experience the transgender sense (but are not guaranteed to). The rational for such probabilistic hypotheses must in part be to try to explain the differences between so-called identical twins.

Continuing, a transcendental explanation for monozygotic twins could be as follows. Identical twins had been close before their current life, perhaps having recently been siblings, close friends, coworkers, or spouses. Such scenarios are consistent with some reports from modern investigations into possible cases of reincarnation [Stevenson, pp.171-172]. This previous closeness brought them together to be born as monozygotic twins and was the underlying cause of the initial split of the single cell zygote. Continuity of behavioral tendencies tends to result in their roughly similar personalities - as is often found between those who are close - and also could provide for some shared behavioral preferences. Their previous connection, perhaps including their shared disembodied experiences, provides a basis for their unbelievable closeness. Superficially, such twins are material-only replicas produced by the same DNA blueprint, but underneath there are two separate beings with mostly separate backgrounds accounting for much of their otherwise surprising differences. The issue of male exclusive homosexuality amongst monozygotic twins will be returned to in a later chapter.

For a Western historical perspective on such views consider the following observations from the 1600s from Joseph Glanvill, Chaplain to King Charles II:

Every soul brings a kind of sense with it into the world, whereby it tastes and relisheth what is suitable to its particular temper .... What can we conclude but that that the soul itself is the immediate subject of all this variety and that it came prejudiced and prepossessed into this body with some implicit notions that it had learned in another? To say that all this [individual] variety proceeds primarily from the mere temper of our bodies is methinks a very poor and unsatisfying account. For those that are the most alike in the temper, air, and complexion of their bodies, are yet of a vastly differing genius [tendencies] .... What then can we conjecture is the cause of all this diversity, but that we had taken a great delight and pleasure in some things like and analogous unto these in a former condition [Head and Cranston, p.122].

Has any modern researcher read or considered such a perspective?

Behavioral Genetics Reconsidered

In one of Steven Pinker's intellectual epics, *The Blank Slate*, he offered some concluding thoughts on the modern intellectual movement characterized by extreme environmental assumptions [Pinker 2002]. This nurture-only perspective in Pinker's opinion "became part of the secular faith and appeared to constitute the common decency of our age". Pinker then summarized the downside, including that this perspective "torments mothers who work outside the home and parents whose children did not turn out as they would have liked" and that it "blinds us to our cognitive and moral shortcomings". He then went on to write that:

[r]egardless of its good and bad effects, the Blank Slate is an empirical hypothesis about the functioning of the brain and must be evaluated in terms of whether or not it is true. The modern sciences of mind, brain, genes,

and evolution are increasingly showing that it is not true [p.421].

Into the intellectual vacuum of that fading movement appears to be a tsunami of its own - the modern DNA-based, bio-robotic vision of life. This biology-based belief views all of life as material-only expressions. In geneticist J. Craig Venter's recent book, *Life at the Speed of Light: From the Double Helix to the Dawn of Digital Life,* Venter's answer to "a question at the heart of biology: 'What is life?'" was provided as "DNA-driven biological machines" [Venter, p.6]. The associated big picture view is of a collection of evolved species-defining DNA pools and the corresponding view of an individual is as the outcome of a lottery-like event within one of those pools. One could argue about some of the unhealthy import of this mechanized view of life - as with regards to the treatment of mental illness - but perhaps it is the overall certainty with which it is pushed that should be most objectionable.

One key line of observations that bolstered the modern faith in the behavioral import of DNA, was studies of monozygotic twins that had been separated in infancy. Observations from such studies were then compared to those from studies of raised-together monozygotic twins and nature-versus-nurture inferences drawn. Specifically, if the differences in a behavioral attribute seen between raised-together and raised-apart twins was small, then the corresponding nurture contribution was also presumed to be small. Also of note here was that the degree of similarity found between the raised-apart twins on a particular behavior (that correlation) was assumed to be an approximation of the corresponding genetic (or nature) contribution. Thus, in a very significant 1990 *Science* article entitled "Sources of Human Psychological Differences: The Minnesota Study of Twins Reared Apart", Thomas J. Bouchard, Jr. *et al* had written:

> [o]ur findings support and extend those from many family, twin, and adoption studies, a broad consilience of findings leading to the following generalization: For almost every behavioral trait so far investigated, from

reaction time to religiosity, an important fraction of the variation among people turns out to be associated with genetic variation [Bouchard et al].

And then more particularly they wrote:

[o]n multiple measures of personality and temperament, occupational and leisure-time interests, and social attitudes, monozygotic twins reared apart are about as similar as are monozygotic twins reared together [Bouchard et al].

The similarity noted here supported the first quote on the behavioral import of DNA. One particular focus in that paper was on intelligence and for that behavior attribute the calculated genetic contribution was "70% of the variance in IQ". Based on such results one might well surmise that we are far from environmentally-defined "blank slates".

Returning to the earlier Pinker quote, his focus on veracity as the bottom line was certainly appropriate. A pillar of the modern materialist vision is that DNA blueprints specify for various individual outcomes. In a general species- and gender-defining sense that import appears quite likely to be the case, although little has been confirmed. For certain specific conditions there are also confirmed DNA origins. (Additionally, in the case of tumors, specific DNA mutations have been found to be driving particular growth dynamics.) But for the broadside of who we are as individuals - including much of the territories staked out by behavioral genetics and personal genomics - the large scientific efforts have identified "almost nothing" and thus the ongoing silence. Also predating DNA searches there have been a number of obvious questions for this materialist view, in particular in the behavioral realm. With the transgender phenomenon, some people do spend their entire lives wishing that they were the opposite sex and a recent study found that many of them who have undergone sex-change efforts (transitioned) "knew they had been born into the wrong gender from childhood?" [Landau]. Did biologists and psychologists really think they were going to find a DNA - or environmental - explanation for this phenomenon?

So what kind of response has this DNA impasse generated? Apparently very little, except perhaps some scrambling around to try to hold down the bio-fort. In a 2011 lonely assessment of the analogous personal genomics situation, Jonathan Latham and Allison Wilson pointed out that with few exceptions (including previously identified genes for cystic fibrosis, sickle cell anemia, and Huntington's disease; and also including genetic contributions for some instances of Alzhemier's and breast cancer):

> according to the best available data, genetic predispositions (i.e. causes) have a negligible role in heart disease, cancer, stroke, autoimmune diseases, obesity, autism, Parkinson's disease, depression, schizophrenia and many other common mental and physical illnesses that are the major killers in Western countries [Latham and Wilson].

They went on to ask (in italics) "[h]ow likely is it that a quantity of genetic variation that could only be called enormous (i.e. more than 90-95% of that for 80 human diseases) is all hiding in what until now [circa 2010] had been considered genetically unlikely places?" Latham and Wilson then conjectured that the missing contributors must be environmental but this appears to be an enormous stretch. Although they might have been right about the potential worth of increasing attention on environmental factors, their neglect of innate contributions doesn't make sense, in particular beginning with the health differences found between monozygotic twins. Nonetheless, Latham and Wilson appropriately pointed out that "[b]y all rights then, reports of the GWA [genome wide assessments] results should have filled the front pages of every world newspaper for a week". Needless to say that big missing heritability coverage hasn't happened.

Rather, the media coverage went another way. For example, in the fall of 2012 there was an avalanche of media stories about big developments from unexpected regions of the DNA. The *New York*

Times reported that the "junk" DNA findings were "considered a major medical and scientific breakthrough, [and have] enormous implications for human health" [Kolata 2012]. Also reported was that one prominent researcher had commented that the junk DNA developments were "a stunning resource" and that his "head explode[d] at the amount of data". The seemingly hyped nature of the junk reports was then confirmed in a very unusual guest blog write-up at *Scientific American*. Biologist Athena Andreadis in a September 17, appropriately titled entry, "Junk DNA, Junk PR", described the origin of the junk DNA reports as "a huge, painstakingly orchestrated PR campaign" by the relevant scientists and that the developments didn't "alter the current view of the genome" [Andreadis]. This criticism appears consistent with the earlier assessment by evolutionary biologists that most of our DNA is in fact nonfunctioning junk. Thus Andreadis' critical comments were apparently representative of the big rift that this resuscitation of junk DNA by geneticists setoff between themselves and evolutionary biologists [Zimmer 2015].

Now returning back to Steven Pinker's *The Blank Slate*, there is a nice section laying out some of the basic findings of behavioral genetics [Pinker 2002, pp.372-381]. The first two laws of behavioral genetics describe the inferred inputs from nature and nurture. In modest fashion he introduced the second of these laws - "[t]he effect of being raised in the same family is smaller than the effect of the genes [i.e., the first law]" [p.373]. This could have been better stated as, "short of traumatic effects and some nominal allegiances (like political affiliation), being raised in the same family has negligible impact". A negligible familial contribution was in fact Pinker's conclusion. Thus the big argument against the Blank Slate (or nurture dominates) hypothesis is that empirical data have suggested that the influence of nurture is in many ways very small.

Continuing, Pinker had written that the Third Law of behavioral genetics claims that "[a] substantial portion of the variation in complex human behavioral traits are not accounted for by the effects of genes or families" [p.373]. This might have been better stated as "a little over half of an individual's particular behavioral tendencies do not make nature plus nurture sense". Thus in a concrete example, an individual's particular behavioral trait - say tendency towards introversion - is likely to only loosely follow from the state of introversion of their parents and also their family environment. Following the apparently standard routine, Pinker formalized the hypothesized origin of this Third Law by calling it the "Unique Environment". This presumed environmental impact - which most tangibly is posited as the individual environmental experience of one identical twin which made it different than the other twin (and the process somehow produces similar outcomes whether the twins were raised together or were separated at birth) - completes the behavioral genetics model. Pinker offered a nice alternative take of the three laws in writing that "identical twins are 50 percent similar whether they are grow up together or apart" [p.381]. He also acknowledged, though, the mystery of this unique environmental contribution with a Bob Dylan-influenced, "something is happening here but we don't know what it is". Note that this same mysteriousness also limits the traction available for the behavioral import of DNA's recently uncovered and hyped sidekick - the epigenome.

Yet despite the unfolding DNA deficit situation, scientific confidence continues as apparently does all of the genetic reasoning and expenditure based on it. As a relevant snippet, one *New York Times* article offered an individual's conflicting experience with genetic testing [Peikoff]. To solidify the analysis the author had gotten opinions from various relevant scientists. One point repeated was that the current genetic testing wasn't thorough enough. One academic pointed out that the tests are "missing 99.9 percent of the letters that make the genome". The genome pioneer J. Craig Venter was quoted in pointing out that Peikoff's conflicting results "are not the least bit surprising" and that "[a]nything short of [whole genome] sequencing is going to be short on accuracy - and even then, there's almost no comprehensive data sets to compare to".

What wasn't touched on in the Piekoff article was the additional significance of 99.9% - an estimate of the DNA equivalence between any individuals. Additionally, how much of the complementary (0.1%) individual-differentiating DNA have science's considerable search efforts already checked? And how likely is it that those DNA searches would have found "almost nothing" to this point?

Returning to Pinker's behavioral genetics coverage we can see that science's explanation of one's particular behavioral tendencies is essentially based on a presumed DNA contribution plus a hypothesized unique environmental impact. So what happens if this missing DNA situation continues on its "almost nothing" trajectory? Will scientists acknowledge and perhaps emphasize what would constitute a profound mystery? Would a scientist write a follow-up article to Pinker's "My Genome, My Self" [Pinker 2009], perhaps one entitled "My Genome, Basically So What?".

Chapter 2

A Collection of
Intelligence Conundrums

The previous chapter briefly touched on the surprising situation facing scientists attempting to account for the variations in human intelligence. For this significant and basic behavioral attribute, DNA searches have only identified about 1 percent of the expected underlying DNA basis (or genetic component) as of the fall of 2012. During the following August a behavioral genetics researcher in reviewing a manuscript of mine acknowledged a resignation similar that to that conveyed in the same 2012 article (i.e., "99 percent empty"). That such a prominent and variable individual feature could well be de-coupled from a basis in DNA is a stunning development. What then made someone like Albert Einstein so intellectually superior?

In that same *New York Times* article discussed in chapter 1, the author David Dobbs had described a new theory in which the DNA dynamic for intelligence was reversed. As mentioned earlier, in that theory proposed by the neurogeneticist of Trinity College Dublin, Kevin Mitchell, intelligence was a big evolutionary winner and thus high intelligence was the evolved standard equipment [Mitchell 2012/07]. The variations found in human intelligence were then proposed to come from the inevitable random mutations found in each of our genomes, with such mutations seen as much more likely to hurt rather than help intellectual abilities. Thus humans with the highest innate intelligences simply had minimal contamination of their intelligence blueprint, while the rest of us suffered significant losses via DNA mutations. More subtly, Mitchell had proposed that the apparent inheritance of intelligence reflected an underlying heritable mutation rate. An individual born into a family with a relatively low rate of random mutations present in their genomes, would tend to have a high IQ. Conversely, an individual born into a family which had a higher rate of random mutations would tend to have a lower IQ.

Mitchell's intelligence proposal raised additional questions, though. How could evolution have resulted in something akin to a genius' intelligence as standard equipment? Does the variability apparent in group (average) intelligences then reflect differences in the average DNA mutation rates found amongst groups? Coincidentally, eight days after the Dobbs article the *New York Times Magazine* contained a lengthy article by Andrew Solomon entitled "How Do You Raise a Prodigy?" [Solomon 2012/10]. In it were descriptions of high intelligence kids who then from Mitchell's proposed perspective would then have carried minimal dumbing mutations. Here then might be descriptions of kids operating close to the proposed default high intelligence state. Here is an excerpt:

> Drew Petersen didn't speak until he was 3 1/2, but his mother, Sue, never believed he was slow. When he was 18 months old, in 1994, she was reading to him and skipped a word, whereupon Drew reached over and pointed to the missing word on the page.

Drew went on apparently to learn to read quite a bit of sheet music on his own, skip the first of six months of formal piano lessons at age 5, and then within the year was "performing Beethoven sonatas at the recital hall at Carnegie Hall". On the way to kindergarten at one point Drew asked his mom, "[c]an I just stay home so I can learn something"? His mom had commented, "[h]e was reading textbooks this big, and they're in class holding up a blowup M". Additionally, Drew and some of the other prodigies considered had exhibited enormous self-determinations which left one mom commenting "it's not for me to be proud; [she] who does this herself".

As conveyed in the prodigy article, such examples of high intelligence appeared to be overwhelmingly innate. Drew's parents did not appear to be standout intellectuals, also had a non-prodigy child, and sensibly seemed to avoid hyping the genius business. But again does such relatively high intelligence make sense as an evolutionary outcome? From an evolutionary standpoint is it even likely to be found in our evolutionary cognitive card collection, let alone as a standard outcome? As previously touched on, a framework for contemplating the evolutionary forces that shaped our intelligence was presented in Steven Pinker's *How the Mind Works* [Pinker 1997, pp.186-190]. That description consisted of humans having found a cognitive niche specializing in how to outsmart and then often eat other species. As described above, Pinker had pointed out life for our "ancestors [was like] a camping trip that never ends" without modern equipment. Pinker had appropriately introduced this concept with a chapter title "Revenge of the Nerds". A simpler evolutionary dynamic was the development of trichromatic vision within our primate heritage which could have been helpful for identifying ripe fruit. But is the proposed cognitive evolutionary dynamic - with natural selection weeding out DNA that was lousy for campings' cognitive tasks and also preserving and spreading some fortuitous DNA camping gems - likely to make possible, let alone standardize the kind of high intelligence exhibited by prodigies? How natural selection could have produced a little kid capable of playing Beethoven sonatas, and being sufficiently self-motivated to do so, is quite the conundrum.

◆ ◆ ◆

The remainder of this chapter considers a collection of three intelligence-related mysteries - a childhood behavioral syndrome, the Einstein Syndrome; the somewhat overlapping phenomena of prodigies and savants; and then the Flynn Effect or the observed historical rise in IQ's. In isolation each of these mysteries provides plenty of puzzlement, but in the context of the lack of DNA support for our variations in intelligence it will be argued that together they represent a very significant challenge to the modern understanding of humans. The material that follows is an updated version of some material presented in a paper published in the medical online journal, Cureus.com in August 2013 [Christopher].

The Einstein Syndrome

Thomas Sowell's book *The Einstein Syndrome - Bright Children Who Talk Late* considered a very interesting behavioral phenomena named for the late physicist Albert Einstein (Sowell is a well known author and economist) [Sowell 2001]. Sowell pointed out that children with this condition have "speech development [which] lags far behind that of other children their age, while their intellectual development surges ahead of their peers" [p.1]. These children often are very strong willed, late in toilet training, relatively weak socially, and their intellectual strengths are focused in analytical areas and/or music. They also tend to possess exceptional memories. Simply put such kids appear to be born quite strongly nerd-inclined ("nerd" is not a slight). Another prominent characteristic is that they are almost always born into families with a strong technical and/or musical presence.

The Einstein Syndrome considered children fitting this description whose parents had come together in two groups. One group represented the experiences of 43 biological families and was connected with Sowell, while the other group represented 232 biological families under the auspices of Professor Stephen Camarata, a speech pathologist at the Vanderbilt University Medical Center [pp.4-5]. With the inclusion of a few families with multiple late-talkers, the respective counts of biological children were, 45 and 236. The median age of beginning to speak in the smaller group connected to Sowell was four years old, while the figure for the children in Professor Camarata's group was three and a half [p.107]. In the smaller group most kids "did not make a statement using more than one word until they were at least three and a half years old and their first complete sentence was spoken when they were four" [pp.17-18].

For comparison, the normal development of speech progresses from single word utterances and then at "around 18 months the child starts to combine single words into two word sentences" [Smith et al]. Subsequently, their "[v]ocabulary typically grows from around 20 words at 18 months to around 200 words at 21 months" [p.304]. Furthermore, the large Stanford-based Terman study (1925-59) of gifted children (with IQ's of about 140 and higher) found they tended to talk earlier than their lower IQ peers [p.472].

Sowell had previously written a book, *Late-Talking Children* [Sowell 1998], on this subject and had a son who had exhibited this syndrome. Professor Camarata also had had a son with this syndrome and he himself had demonstrated it as well. Almost 90% of the children in these groups were boys [Sowell 2001, pp.9-10]. Also noteworthy was that 26 percent of the children in Sowell's group had a close relative who had exhibited this syndrome, while the corresponding figure for Camarata's group was 48 percent [p.9].

A "striking" characteristic found with the Einstein Syndrome was that the associated families "are highly atypical - and highly analytical" in their occupations [Sowell 2001, p.5]. Of the late-talking children considered, almost three quarters "had at least one close relative who was either an engineer, a scientist, or a mathematician" [p.5]. Close relatives in this context were limited to parents, grandparents, aunts, uncles, and additionally for Camarata's group, siblings. The children in the two study groups were about 10 times as likely to have fathers who were engineers as were late-talking children in general that had been considered in a British study [p.7]. It is noteworthy that this association with a family type perhaps mirrors a weaker correlation observed between the occurrence of autism and technical families considered by Simon Baron-Cohen in a November 2012 *Scientific American* article.

Also observed was also a big musical connection. In both groups about three-fourths of the kids had a close relative who played a musical instrument. In Camarata's group 28% of them had a close relative who was a professional musician and in Sowell's group that figure was 26% [Sowell 2001, pp.7-8]. This appeared to be another relatively focused activity correlated with the occurrence of this syndrome within a family.

Some of the stories involving these children exhibiting the Einstein Syndrome were amazing. In one instance the three year old "silent" son of a professor was involved in the following:

> The older boy, now five, had learned to read and would entertain his doting parents by doing so aloud. One evening he came upon a word he did not recognize, and struggled with it. At which point his brother toddled over, peered at the text and read out the sentence perfectly. Following that, he again lapsed into silence for several months and only then began to speak easily [p.19].

In another case a toddler "became deeply absorbed in listening to Bach, to the point of being moved to tears" [p.85]. Sowell also wrote that "one of the five-year-old pre-schoolers in my group helped both his mother at home and his teacher at school when they had problems using the computer (circa the 1990's). He could also play the piano with his eyes closed" [p.12]. Extraordinary child lock breaking abilities were exhibited by Sowell's own son prior to the age of one [p.41].

In a detour from Sowell's *The Einstein Syndrome* coverage, the earlier considered prodigy Drew Petersen appeared to fit the syndrome profile in so far as demonstrating the late-talking attribute and also in having an engineer for a father [Solomon 2012/10]. As described in Solomon's book, one of Drew's piano teachers later recalled her reaction to hearing him for the first time:

> [he] could barely reach the pedals, but played with every adult nuance you'd ever want. I thought, 'Oh my

God, this really is a genius. He's not mimicking and not being spoon-fed. His musicality comes from within.' [Solomon 2012, p.418]

Thomas Sowell also considered some earlier experiences of adults who apparently had had the syndrome (including Albert Einstein). One was the pianist Arthur Rubenstein who demonstrated a remarkable draw to the piano as a young child:

[he] became fixated on the piano. Whenever he was asked to leave the drawing room where [it] was kept he screamed and wept. He began playing the piano at age three. When his father later brought him a violin to play, little Arthur reacted by smashing it, earning himself a spanking [Sowell 2001, p.39].

Sowell wrote that such strong-willed behavior "will be all too familiar" to Einstein Syndrome parents. Further Rubenstein:

[a]fter hearing a performance of the first suite of Edvard Grieg's *Peer Gynt*, [he] returned home 'to play almost all of it - to the amazement of the family'. At this point Rubenstein was not yet five years old and had not yet begun formal instruction under a professional musician. At age seven, he gave his first public performance [p.40].

Another remarkable developmental syndrome, Williams Syndrome (roughly the opposite of the Einstein Syndrome), was also touched on.

These amazing behaviors led Sowell to title his explanatory chapter, "Groping for Answers". There he carefully laid out some hypotheses about possible brain developmental dynamics which could have produced the specific patterns of the observed aptitudes. Beneath this he favored a DNA/heredity basis with some support coming from the earlier occurrences of the syndrome amongst close relatives and also indirectly by the analytical-orientations of the families.

Within families with instances of the Einstein Syndrome most other siblings were normally developing, though [Sowell 2001, p.97 and epilogue]. Additionally, of course, most high aptitude technical and/or musical people have not followed this pattern. Given the rarity of the syndrome a DNA explanation would seem likely to involve some form of a mutation, but is it realistic for a mutation to produce this set of behaviors? Is it plausible for a bio-molecular code to specify for a particular obsession such as with the piano? Additionally, how could the relevant mutations be localized to this type of family?

A possible explanation from the transcendental perspective is as follows. A being who became highly focused in a previous technical and/or musically-occupied life was reborn and brought along some of their behavioral tendencies and capabilities. This behavioral skew was also carried over and reflected in their brain as well and this combination could have contributed to the delayed speech. Additionally, a symptom associated with a person being very intellectually focused is that they also tend to be out of touch with their body and this could have been reflected in the phenomenon of delayed toilet training. The fact that such children were predominantly found in technical and/or musically-connected families reflected the tendency of an incarnating-being to be drawn to similar and/or previously-related parents. From this perspective, one might expect that this syndrome would not be found within cultures that do not support analogous careers. Have there been any Albert Einstein's born in groups that don't support scientific-like careers (or more generally distant from such groups)?

The above transcendental take on the Einstein Syndrome portrays some basic elements of a possible transcendental dynamic in which the incarnating soul tends to be drawn to local, similar, and/or previously-related parents. This dynamic would be consistent with the crude heredity patterns that underlie DNA expectations, for example in the field of behavioral genetics. Further, although the The Einstein Syndrome did not report on measured brain characteristics, it is likely that the children exhibiting these unusual characteristics also had correlated brain features. Likewise, there have been observations from brain imaging studies in which some features apparently connected to high intelligence stood out, yet the observed correlation between intelligence scores and variations in DNA is again only about 1 percent [Zimmer 2008, Dobbs]. This could be viewed as an example of a transcendental Lamarckian-like effect. With such a transcendental dynamic a very focused individual could then pass on some of their acquired characteristics to their next incarnation, as opposed to their offspring as was proposed with the Lamarkian evolutionary dynamic. Such a transcendental Lamarckian dynamic might also involve the production of supporting mutations as was suggested for the cause of the initial zygotic split leading to monozygotic twins. (Also of note here is that the Lamarkian concept has been scientifically resuscitated in connection with possible epigenetic inheritance effects).

Finally on a potentially related note, bright children are much more likely to experience myopia [Sowell 2001, p.90] and among autistic or retarded musical prodigies "a majority ... have been either congenitally blind or severely visually impaired" [p.102]. Sowell had used these points in part as supportive of a heredity-based explanation for the Einstein Syndrome. From a transcendental perspective such visual impairments could be viewed as symptomatic of rebirths that were extremely focused on music and thus involved corresponding losses of neglected capacities.

Savants

The second challenge considered here involves the behavior of savants as depicted in Darold A. Treffert's very interesting book, *Islands of Genius* [Treffert 2010]. In addition to traditional autistic savants this book also considered the recently recognized acquired savant syndrome in which savant behavior appears in the wake of a central nervous system setback. Although not considered here, Treffert's book also considered sudden savant syndrome in which savant skills seem to appear spontaneously. Treffert's preface provided the following introductions to some of the savant terrain:

> Kim Peek, the inspiration for the movie Rain Man, memorized 12,000 books. He is the Mt. Everest of memory with bottomless factual recall in multiple areas of expertise including history, geography, literature, music, sports, science and religion, to name only some. He became a living Google. But as a child, his parents were advised to put him in an institution. One doctor suggested a lobotomy.
>
> Matt Savage, who couldn't stand noise or being touched as a child, very quickly mastered the piano at age 6 1/2 and had his first CD of jazz composition at age eight. Matt is recognized worldwide now as "the Mozart of Jazz," a title conferred on him by the famous jazz artist Dave Brubeck. At age 17 he is the leader of the Matt Savage Trio, giving concerts around the globe. He recently recorded his eighth CD.
>
> Leslie Lemke is blind, severely cognitively impaired and has cerebral palsy. Yet he played Tchaikovsky's Piano Concerto No. 1 flawlessly after hearing it for the first time at age 14. Leslie, who has never had a music lesson in his life, is a musical genius.
>
> After a 15-minute helicopter ride over London, Stephen Wiltshire, in a five-day drawing marathon, produced a spectacularly accurate four meter long sketch which captures with mind-boggling fidelity seven square miles of London - building by building, street by street, window by window. Diagnosed with autism at age three, he was described as a "rocket of young talent" on the scene at age eight. Stephen was invested by Queen Elizabeth II as a Member of the Order of the British

Empire and now has his own gallery in the Royal Opera Arcade in London.

These extraordinary people, and others like them ... have savant syndrome, a rare but remarkable condition in which incredible abilities - "islands of genius" - coexist side by side, in jarring juxtaposition, to certain disabilities within the same person [pp.XIII-XIV].

Also in the preface Treffert suggested that:

no model of brain function, including memory, will be complete until it can fully incorporate and explain this jarring contradiction of extraordinary ability and sometimes permeating disability in the same person. Until we can fully explain the savant, we cannot fully explain ourselves nor comprehend our full capacities [p.XIV].

For Treffert there appeared to be no doubt that these remarkable behaviors arose solely from physical processes in the brain. The central mystery for him was the origins of those savant-functioning capabilities. His explanation involved what he called "genetic memory" and in particular that savants have somehow tapped into our shared DNA-based storage of knowledge and skills and then implemented them in the hardware of their brain. He thus offered a technical analogy of the factory-installed software on a computer. His specific storage vehicle was the epigenome, the conditioned side-kick of the genome (via molecules effecting the enfoldment of the genome's packaging or chromatin).

In about half of the cases savant syndrome occurred concurrently with an autistic disorder and in the rest the underlying disorder was a brain injury or disease. Of particular interest were the prodigious savants whom Treffert believed would have been characterized as geniuses or prodigies if they didn't have the coexisting disability. In this regard there is some overlap here with Einstein Syndrome.

Some distinguishing characteristics of prodigious savants include extraordinary memories and also exceptional but narrowly focused skills. Such savants are believed to be very rare with "probably fewer than 100 known prodigious savants living worldwide" [p.25]. Treffert described five areas that the skills of savants appear to focus on - calendar calculating (usually finding the day of the week associated with a specified date), music, art, mathematical and number skills (including super-fast calculations), and mechanical or spatial skills [pp.19-22].

Treffert detailed some of the brain changes that have been found to be associated with savant syndrome [Treffert 2010, pp.48-54]. These typically involve some damage to the left hemisphere and then subsequent compensatory changes and efforts on the part of the brain's right hemisphere. Here is his somewhat concise description:

> disruption of typical left hemisphere function from prenatal influences - such as detrimental hormonal effects on the cortex from circulating testosterone - or other injurious prenatal, perinatal or postnatal development in children and adolescents, or from later brain injury or disease in adults. These injuries produce compensatory right brain skills and abilities to offset left brain dominance. In addition there is, simultaneously, probably from those same detrimental factors, injury to the cortico-limbic (cognitive or semantic memory) circuits with substitution and reliance on (habit or procedural) memory circuits. This combination of left brain and cortico-limbic circuitry damage, with compensatory right brain skills and reliance on habit and procedural memory, produces the clinical picture that is savant syndrome [p. 54].

That there are corresponding changes in the brain is perhaps only part of the functional story. Was the memory exhibited by Stephen Wiltshire after his 15 minute helicopter ride or Kim Peek's book recall really feasible with a brain-only realization? In the *Blank*

Slate Steven Pinker pointed out the intuitive when he wrote that "learning *is* a change in some part of the brain" [Pinker 2002, p.45]. You can sense this when you try to memorize a phone number or more subtly as you acquire a new habit. But can the biology of the human brain provide the extremely rapid changes implied by the recalls exhibited by Kim Peek and Stephen Wiltshire?

Another striking memory feat presented by Treffert came from Oliver Sacks' book, *An Anthropologist on Mars*. It involved a man named Franco Magnani who experienced a serious but unknown illness which had effects including "delirium" and "perhaps seizures" [Treffert 2010, pp.198-199]. After recovering "Magnani began painting immaculately accurate scenes from the village of Pontito [Italy] where he had grown up, but had left at age 18." In addition to the "digital-fidelity recall" the painting skills and interest appeared to come out of the blue. Magnani was quoted, "Fantastic. How could I do it? And how could I have had the gift and not known about it before?". Other examples of "massive autobiographical memory" or hyperthymesic syndrome were also given. Again does such memory seem brain-only feasible? What about the associated energy demands?

In an apparent parallel, observations of non-savants with hyperthymesic phenomena was the focus of a February 2014 *Scientific American* article, "Remembrance of All Things Past" [McGaugh and LePort]. That article opened with an excerpt from an e-mail that the lead author James McGaugh had received from a woman named Jill Price:

> As I sit here trying to figure out where to begin explaining why I am writing you ... I just hope somehow you can help me. I am 34 years old, and since I was 11 I have had this unbelievable ability to recall my past ... I can take a date, between 1974 and today, and tell you what day it falls on, what I was doing that day, and if anything of great importance ... occurred on that day I can describe that to you as well. I do not look at

calendars beforehand, and I do not read 24 years of my journals either.

The authors then followed up and extensively tested Price's recall of events and her memory was eventually proved faulty in one case - the day of the week of one of the previous 23 Easters (and Price is Jewish). Along the way she "corrected the book of milestones for the date of the start of the Iran hostage crisis at the U.S. embassy in 1979". During tests of less significant dates Price:

> correctly recalled that Bing Crosby died at a golf course in Spain on October 14, 1977. When asked how she knew, she replied that when she was 11 years old, she heard the announcement of Crosby's death over the car radio when her mother was driving her to a soccer game [note there must be an error or typo in the article since Price couldn't have been 11 years old in both 1974 and 1977].

She demonstrated an "immediate recall of the day of the week for any date in her life after she was about 11 years old". Yet she "has trouble remembering which of her keys go into which lock" and "does not excel in memorizing facts by rote". The remainder of McGaugh and LePort's article chronicled their subsequent confirmation of similar extraordinary memories in about 50 people. Such memories were found to be "highly organized in that they are associated with a particular day and date" and that it occurred "naturally and without exertion". The authors also did not find evidence that the phenomena tended to have a family history and thus some implied support for a genetic explanation. In any case, such phenomenal memories could be prompting some basic questioning amongst neuroscientists and others.

Back to Darold Treffert's *Islands of Genius* where substantial efforts involved trying to account for the mysterious savant learning. The examples given in the book appeared to strongly support his contention that "they indeed know things [and exhibit skills] that they never learned" [Treffert 2010, p.59]. In a 2014

Scientific American article Treffert stated that "[b]y 2010 I had assembled a worldwide registry of 319 known savants, of whom only 32 had the acquired form" [Treffert 2014]. In that article he concluded that "[a]cquired savantism provides strong evidence that a deep well of brain potential resides within us all". In his *Islands of Genius* book he wrote that he believes that the epigenome (in particular as optimistically portrayed in the *NOVA* TV episode, "Ghost in Your Genes") is the vehicle for such transmission and claimed simply "[b]ottom line: genetic memory exists" [Treffert 2010, pp.60-61]. There do not appear to be reports suggesting anything like this capability is plausible, though, and in fact researcher Eric Nestler acknowledged in an interview with *Scientific American* that any epigenetic inheritance effect is "controversial" [Nestler podcast].

I detour here into some descriptive content on the epigenome as it is relevant to Treffert's genetic memory claim (and to some other extraordinary claims). A fine description of what is known of the epigenome, its mechanics, and possible mental health implications can be found in Eric Nestler's *Scientific American* article, "Hidden Switches in the Mind" [Nestler]. The epigenome consists of the additional chemical markers which can indirectly effect the expression of genes by changing the packaging of the encompassing DNA (together the folded-up DNA and its supporting proteins are called chromatin). In particular, if the epigenetic markings influence the shape of the chromatin in such a way that some of the genes are tightly packaged (or tucked away) and thus not readable by RNA, then the expression (or copying) of those genes will be minimized (or switched off). In general as Nestler pointed out, "[t]he environment can influence gene activity by regulating the behavior of epigenetic writers and erasers - and thus the tagging, and restructuring, of chromatin". This packaging dynamic appears to be part of normal genetic functioning - as for example in differentiating the gene expressions found in different cell types (i.e., liver cells versus muscle cells). This epigenetic dynamic also appears capable of long-term, unhealthy, conditioned impacts as potentially with addictions and mental illnesses. The potential for any heritable effects - and thus conceivably with prodigal inexplicable learning - is difficult to imagine, though.

Treffert's confidant claim - "bottom line: genetic memory exists" - would presumably entail the recording and downloading of complex neural patterns believed to embody high level learning to the germ line's (or germ cell's) epigenome; the subsequent reproductive passage of that enfoldment; and ultimately the uploading of that epigenetic encoding to the appropriate neural circuits to realize the otherwise inexplicable learning. More subtly, such epigenetic encoding would presumably have to not interfere with normal epigenetic functioning and as part of this survive the two-fold stripping of epigenetic marks that is believed to accompany the reproductive process. If this weren't challenging enough, there would still have to be a historical reproductive lineage to support the specific learning. To explain Jay, the previously considered cello-playing prodigy, via such a "genetic memory" theory, you would still have to identify one or more ancestors who were involved with cello-playing and composing. As Treffert pointed out, though, in the realm of prodigious savants there are some in which there appear to be no "family history of special skills" [Treffert 2010, pp.37-39]. More generally, Treffert's optimism about the possibility of most or all of us having access to such epigenetic-encoded genius is highly unlikely from this perspective as there have been so few intellectually exceptional individuals in history (and unlike bacteria we can't simply transfer our DNA).

Before considering a possible transcendental take on some of the savant phenomena some comments on the principal source here, The Tibetan Book of the Dead (TBD), are in order [Fremantle and Trungpa]. This book was apparently written in the 8th century by a Buddhist religious teacher named Padmasambhava and it contains instructions to aid a dying or recently deceased person in dealing with the presumed subsequent (post-death) intermediate or bardo state. This text was thus often read at the bedsides of the dying or recently deceased. The intermediate state was believed to be quuite tumultuous but it also offered great potential to at minimum secure a good rebirth. The coauthor and late Tibetan teacher Chogyam Trungpa offered a modern synopsis in his commentary:

> there is something which continues, there is the continuity of your positive relationship with your friends and the [religious or spiritual] teaching, so work on that basic continuity, which has nothing to do with the ego. When you die you will have all sorts of traumatic experiences, of leaving the body, as well as your old memories coming back to you as hallucinations. Whatever the visions and hallucinations may be, just relate to what is happening rather than trying to run away. Keep there, just relate with that [p.40].

Trungpa's commentary also emphasized an interpretation of underlying energies in the bardos. Another Tibetan teacher, Tulku Thondup, characterized the bardo experience as "like a dream journey, fabricated by our own habitual mental impressions" [Thondup, p.10]. Much of the TBD involves very explicit suggestions in particular to help the deceased realize their own ultimate nature and alternatively to simply avoid a bad rebirth (and written apparently for those with Tibetan Buddhist-flavored "habitual mental impressions"). The intentionality of the soul within the bardo is viewed as a key and thus the repeated instructions to maintain an altruistic attitude dedicated to the betterment of "all sentient beings".

It is the associated description of the post-death or bardo soul that is of particular interest here. It is stated several times that "in the bardo state the mind becomes nine times more clear" and also that the associated memory is such that even if the TBD was "heard ... only once and the meaning not understood" then after death "it will be remembered with not even a single word forgotten" [Fremantle and Trungpa, pp.167-168]. This claimed clarity and memory capability, though, would presumably compete against the claimed "visions and hallucinations".

A crude transcendental explanation of savant syndrome could then begin with simple transcendental continuity and thus the inexplicable learning and interests were carried over from past lives. More particularly, if a person had been very interested and strongly habituated to an activity such as music then that tendency might continue in the intermediate state and ultimately result in a rebirth with very focused behavioral tendencies. In a physics-sense they caught a resonance and this carried over strongly into their subsequent life. Perhaps such a process could allow for some of the underlying "nine times more clear" soul-mind to shine through in a focused way and thus produce some of the spectacular prodigious savant feats. Analogously, the acquired savant syndrome could reflect neural setbacks that inadvertently opened a window for the functioning of the underlying soul-mind. On this note the similarity between some pre-epiletic seizure experiences (involving an "intense heightening of awareness" and not "abnormal or fantastic visions") and some transcendental mystical awakening experiences [Sekida, pp.14-15] could then be literal and not neural-only phenomena (including of course hallucinations [Sachs]).

Finally, an additional very specific bardo description and possible savant connection comes from Tulku Thondup's book, *Peaceful Death, Joyful Rebirth* [Thondup]. In it he wrote that:

> [s]ome people relive their dying experiences, exactly as they went through them, on every seventh day after their death, again and again, especially if it was a tragic death. That is why every seventh day is observed by survivors with prayers and dedications [p.88].

Facing such a scenario would likely whittle down your perspective on things and strongly frame time in a cycle-of-7 (or modulo 7) days perspective. With savant syndrome the most common - "almost universally, present" - unusual ability and focus is with calendar calculating. This phenomena apparently is also present amongst hyperthymesic individuals (and such individuals also "scored higher on a test of obsessive personality traits"). Why and how this calendar calculating happens is an enormous mystery.

Central to it appears to be a fixation on time through a day of the week (or modulo 7) perspective.

The Flynn Effect

The third and final mystery considered here is the Flynn Effect. Philosopher James Flynn (and some less noted earlier researchers) noticed that IQ scores in many countries appeared to be rising during the twentieth century [Pinker 2011, Folger]. Although there is no shortage of controversy here, the apparent rising IQ's are not in question. The "bombshell" as Steven Pinker put it "is that the Flynn Effect is almost certainly environmental" [Pinker 2011, p.653]. How such an environmental dynamic could have evaded previous studies - and everyday perception - of intelligence is truly amazing.

The apparent intelligence gains are not subtle:

> [a]n average teenager today, if he or she could time-travel back to 1950, would have an IQ of 118. If the teenager went back to 1910, he or she would have had an IQ of 130, besting 98 percent of his or her contemporaries. Yes, you [read] that right: if we take the Flynn Effect at face value, a typical person today is smarter than 98 percent of the people in the good old days of 1910. To state it in an even more jarring way, a typical person of 1910, if time-transported forward to the present, would have a mean IQ of 70, which is at the border of mental retardation. With the Raven's Progressive Matrices, a test that is sometimes considered the purest measure of general intelligence, the rise is even steeper. An ordinary person of 1910 would have an IQ of 50 today, which is smack in the middle of mentally retarded territory, between "moderate" and "mild" retardation [Pinker 2011, p.651].

The underlying gains have been largely in the abstract reasoning portions of intelligence tests such as those containing similarities, analogies, and visual patterns (including Raven's Matrices). Little if any gains occurred in the traditional main topics of education - knowledge, math, and vocabulary [Folger; Pinker 2011, p.651]. Thus, arguments connecting these gains to improvements in schooling appear to be inadequate.

Flynn feels that these increases in IQ scores reflect a pervasive shift in modern societies towards more focus on abstract reasoning [Flynn; Pinker 2011, pp.653-654); Folger]. In particular, Flynn hypothesized that this shift involved "scientific reasoning" infiltrating "everyday thinking" on an increasingly wide scale [Flynn; Pinker 2011, p.655]. Steven Pinker offered an explanation - albeit perhaps an optimistic one - that many modern people have apparently "assimilated hundreds of these [scientific] abstractions from casual reading, conversation, and exposure to the media, including *proportional, percentage, correlation, causation, control group, placebo, representative sample, false positive, empirical, post hoc, statistical, median, variability, circular argument, tradeoff,* and *cost-benefit analysis*" [Pinker 2011, p.655]. With such a hypothesized modern shift towards abstraction, Flynn suggested that "we developed new cognitive skills and the kind of brain that can deal with them" [Flynn].

The mystery associated with the Flynn Effect is how this could have happened given the relatively fixed nature of an individual's intelligence quotient. As intelligence researcher Linda Gottfredson put it, "decades of genetics research have shown, ... [that] genetic [or innate] endowments are responsible for much of the variation in mental ability among individuals" [Gottfredson 1999]. Additionally, Gottfredson pointed out that:

> [A]lthough shared environments do have a modest influence on IQ in childhood, their effects dissipate by adolescence. The IQs of adopted children, for example, lose all resemblance to those of their adoptive family

members and become more like those of the biological parents they have never known.

Certainly some adoptions - perhaps particularly international ones - would seem to have realized in an environmental-sense something akin to the time-travel hypothesized by Pinker. So why hasn't the Flynn Effect also been apparent via some of the environmental dynamics experienced by some individuals?

Additionally, the limited real-world import of these apparent gains in aptitude was vividly suggested by Linda Gottfredson's citing of the complexity barriers encountered in a 1993 literacy survey of American adults [Gottfredson 2012]. Included was the observation that only 17 percent were able to use "a bus schedule to determine the appropriate bus for a given set of conditions" and only 3 percent were able to "answer the most complex questions, like determining the total cost of carpet to cover a room (using a calculator)".

Nonetheless, the puzzling gains in our aptitude for abstract reasoning beg an explanation. From a transcendental perspective this could be explained as a Lamarckian-like effect due to the increased emphasis on abstract reasoning in the modern world. From this perspective there has been a transcendental boost in innate abstract reasoning abilities as souls have cycled thru (human) lives with more and more emphasis on abstraction. This would be similar to the earlier proposed explanations for the gains found with the Einstein Syndrome and savants, but without the large focal boosts. This would also be consistent with the innate intelligence differences found between individuals (and group averages), differences which so far have been minimally correlated with DNA. Thus the differences in the intellectual demands, possibilities, and pursuits across transcendental trajectories could have produced different cumulative Lamarckian-like contributions to the innate intellectual capacities of individuals. If Gottfredson's complexity example is representative, though, the hypothesized transcendental boost in aptitudes has not been matched by a critical boost in intellectual motivations.

In any case such a transcendental process would place the environmental influence for contemporary intelligence score gains in the previous lives of individuals, with the most recent life perhaps being the dominant contributor. The alternative of trying to account for contemporary gains amidst modern society's increasingly distracted norms and reduced physical activity is difficult. Flynn in fact commented, "[t]o my amazement, in the 21st century the increases are continuing" and went on to add, "as if guided by an invisible hand" [Folger].

Discussion on Intelligence and its Conundrums

A prominent feature of any human being is their intelligence. This might be the biggest item on the behavioral genetics queue. In some cases an individual's intelligence really stands out, somewhat analogous to extremes in height. The basis of the variations in this basic human feature was supposed to be largely found in DNA, even apparently in the cases of exceptionally high intelligence. The inability to confirm that DNA basis is certainly a big deal and a good example of the missing heritability problem. Given the significance of the development of intelligence in our evolutionary history as evidenced by our much increased brain size, scientists certainly must have expected to find a number of pieces of DNA supporting that species dynamic (and initial support was described in [Pollard]) and further for its variation amongst individuals.

Does the explanation involving a default high level of intelligence with the variations being imposed in a downward fashion via random mutations seem plausible? A look at the remarkable high intelligence terrain poses immediate challenges to that explanation. Even without the particular conundrum of inexplicable learning, it is difficult to imagine how our evolutionary history could have resulted in codes for such high levels. At the very least the mysteries associated with our intellectual abilities should receive more recognition in scientific circles and be more commonly communicated to the public. The usual sense of certainty associated with scientific materialism should give way to an acknowledgement of some of these mysteries.

In another relevant academic area, one would think that philosophers would be jumping on such mysteries, particularly ones so close to knowledge. With the exception of one philosopher (who had demonstrated the temerity to argue for the existence of free will), though, none of my efforts to pass on this intellectual tip produced any response from the realm of philosophy. Moreover, I have seen no evidence that any philosopher is pursuing anything connected to the unfolding DNA mystery. Not too long ago as evidenced by the work in [Head and Cranston] some philosophers wondered about a possible transcendental process and its heritable implications. Also from studying possible cases of reincarnation, Stevenson and Tucker naturally wondered some about those implications [Stevenson; Tucker 2005. See for example the closing chapters].

My own perspective on the transcendental hypothesis has been somewhat conjoined to my interest in Buddhism. There must certainly have been numerous other earlier beliefs on the nature of a possible transcendental process, although perhaps only a few of them are still available in the modern world. On this point, I introduce some descriptions of the soul as possibly relevant to a transcendental explanation. In the *Tibetan Book of the Dead* there is a duality in such descriptions between a passive (or "emptiness") aspect and an active (or "luminosity") aspect. Here is an excerpt describing the disembodied post-death state:

> [t]hese two, your mind whose nature is emptiness without any substance whatever, and your mind which is vibrant and luminous, are inseparable: this is the dharmakaya of the buddha. This mind of yours is inseparable luminosity and emptiness in the form of a great mass of light, it has no birth or death ... [Fremantle and Trungpa, p.87]

This appears to be an elemental description of the underlying transcendental soul. Of note in this depiction is that I am avoiding the longstanding muddled self-versus-no-self philosophical debate which entertains some Buddhists (although this certainly doesn't appear to describe a non-self).

Somewhat of a complement to the TBD can be found in the far-ranging and earnest discussions of the book *I AM THAT* based on talks with the late Indian teacher Nisargadatta. These discussions, like Nisargadatta, had a somewhat loose affiliation with the Hindu tradition. That tradition includes teachings from both a top-down or God perspective and also a bottom-up or soul perspective. In any case, the emphasis in those discussions appeared to be in moving towards a direct experience of - and hopefully ongoing foothold in - the soul's perspective (and thus the title of the book). Briefly, the depicted very big challenge was to maintain close observations of living experiences so as to appreciate phenomena as-is, without getting caught up in memory-based detours. Here is a simple subjectively-oriented excerpt in which Nisargadatta answered a question on personal differences:

> [t]here is no difference between us; nor can I say that I know myself, I know that I am not describable nor definable. There is a vastness beyond the farthest reaches of the mind [i.e., workings of the brain]. That vastness is my home; that vastness is myself. And that vastness is also love [Nisargadatta, p.530].

Chapter 3

Animal Mysteries

The previously mentioned disconnect between DNA and longevity also appears to be true in the case of some animals. In Steven Pinker's *The Blank Slate* in an effort to support a possible random explanation of the Third Law of behavioral genetics (given the enormous complexity of the human brain), Pinker wrote that:

> [o]ne roundworm may live three times as long as its virtual clone in the next dish. The biologist Steven Austad commented on the roundworms' lifespans: "Astonishingly, the degree of variability they exhibit in longevity is not much less than that of a genetically mixed population of humans, who eat a variety of diets, attend to or abuse their health, and are subject to all the vagaries of circumstance - car crashes, tainted beef, enraged postal workers - of modern industrialized life". And a roundworm has 959 cells! [Pinker 2002, p.397]

Perhaps also similar to that surprisingly experienced by genetically-identical humans with limited environmental differentiation. A certain amount of randomness associated with the realization of the DNA blueprint is a given. Even the most ardent materialist couldn't have expected monozygotic twins to have identical freckle patterns. But a big random explanation, though, either for the behavioral differences between monozygotic twins or for the longevity variance experienced by laboratory roundworms, undermines the basic mechanical logic of evolution and could also threaten an organism's viability. Also randomness does not relieve the heredity-based expectations on DNA.

Whatever their origins, though, surprising behavioral and personality mysteries amongst animals are also increasingly being noted by scientists. One interesting behavioral example was reported in a *Wildlife Conservation* article entitled "Phantom of the Forest" [Ruggiero]. The author, Richard Ruggiero, reported on a 250 pound young male Western Lowland Gorilla visiting a small village in the Republic of Congo. The gorilla became known to the villagers as "The Phenomenon" or "Ebobo" and it would regularly show up and sit and observe the village, or even walk through it. This was astounding behavior to the villagers and resident wildlife biologists. One of Ebobo's routines involved sitting along a trail and watching the village children walk to school. Biologist Mike Fay pointed out that, "Ebobo is not only the first habituated Western Lowland Gorilla, he is the first self-habituated Western Lowland Gorilla". Some of the villagers felt Ebobo "was a person who had transformed himself into a gorilla or a reincarnation of a deceased villager who had returned home". What kind of a scientific explanation is available here?

Possible support from investigations into reincarnation cases can be found in that a number of the children who experienced apparent explicit recall of a previous life also made repeated requests to return to their previous home. From Jim Tucker's *Life Before Life*, "some cry on an almost daily basis to go back to their family" [Tucker 2005, p.93]. Such requests often became a significant annoyance for their parents. Nonetheless, in some of these cases the children succeeded in getting back to their claimed previous home; re-establishing a connection and getting acceptance with their claimed ex-family; and then subsequently visiting them regularly.

One Thai boy, Chanai Choomalaiwong, had been born in 1967 and as a 3 year old claimed to have been a schoolteacher who had been shot and killed in his previous life (this was consistent with many of the possible reincarnation cases in that the remembered life ended unexpectedly and violently) [Tucker 2005, pp.55-56 and p.145]. Before he turned 4 years old, Chanai's grandmother (and guardian) took him via bus back to the vicinity Chanai had identified, and Chanai then led the way to a house and upon entry identified what he felt were his previous parents. The elderly couple had had a schoolteacher son who had been shot and killed in 1962. Chanai's knowledge of their son's life plus his own birthmarks which appeared consistent with the fatal wound led to a subsequent re-invite. Chanai then returned and recognized additional (previous) family members and gained acceptance as the incarnate of their former relative. Subsequently, he visited regularly and sometimes would even covertly visit them by bus.

The reemerging study of animal personalities has also been uncovering mysteries. In a *New York Times Magazine* article entitled "The Animal Self", George Siebert presented some cases displaying the remarkable variations in personality found amongst animals [Siebert]. The article opened with some observations of the personalities of Giant Pacific Octopuses (G.P.O.) at the Seattle Aquarium. Observations of these animals, which have a lifespan of about 3 or 4 years, included:

> Emily Dickinson, for example, a particularly shy, retiring female G.P.O. who always hid behind the tank's rock outcroppings, or Leisure Suit Larry, who, ... would have been arrested in our world for sexual assault, with his arms always crawling all over passing researchers. And ... Lucretia McEvil [who] repeatedly tore her tank apart at night, scraping up all the rocks at the base, pulling up the water filter, biting through nylon cables ...

Further aquarium observations included,

> One particularly temperamental G.P.O. so disliked having his tank cleaned, he would keep grabbing the cleaning tools, trying to pull them into the tank, his skin going bright red. Another took to regularly soaking one of the aquarium's female night biologists with the water

funnel octopuses normally use to propel themselves, because he didn't like it when she shined her flashlight into his tank.

How much of this behavior makes nature-plus-nurture or scientific sense? Does it seem feasible that Leisure Suit Larry and Lucretia McEvil got their particular behavioral inclinations from some combination of their evolution-shaped DNA and their environmental experiences (plus possible randomness in the growth and layout of their brains)?

The Siebert article considered studies of animals all the way down to insects. In addition to the big variation in personalities, researchers have noted a number of common elements or dimensions in the personalities present in a number of species. Also of note were observations of evolutionary "stupid behaviors". Some seemingly "stupid" examples involving big felines were reported on in a *Wildlife Conservation* article, "Meow Mix" [Jackson]. The wildlife researchers reported on cases of big cats with unusual prey preferences. One of these involved a male Siberian tiger that repeatedly hunted down and killed adult grizzly bears. The researchers tracked the tiger through 8 such kills including what was apparently an epic battle. Why the apparent insistence on such demanding prey?

A 2010 *New York Times* article by Natalie Angier provided somewhat of an update on George Siebert's earlier report on the study of animal personalities [Angier 2010]. From the opening of Angier's "Even Among Animals: Leaders, Followers, and Schmoozers",

> [in] the burgeoning field of animal personality research, the effort to understand why individual members of the same species can be so mulishly themselves, and so unlike one another on a wide variety of behavioral measures. Scientists studying animals from virtually every niche of the bestial kingdom have found evidence of distinctive personalities - bundled sets of behaviors, quirks, preferences and pet peeves that remain stable

over time and across settings. They have found stylistic diversity in chimpanzees, monkeys, barnacle geese, farm minks, blue tits and great tits, bighorn sheep, dumpling squid, pumpkinseed sunfish, zebra finches, spotted hyenas, even spiders and water striders, to name but a few. They have identified hotheads and tiptoers, schmoozers and loners, divas, dullards and fearless explorers, and they have learned that animals, like us, often cling to the same personality for the bulk of their lives. The daredevil chicken of today is the one out crossing the road tomorrow.

Researchers are delving into the source and significance of all these animal spirits.

Over some objections the animal psychology researchers feel that these tendencies warrant the term "personality". Also of note was mention that some preliminary research suggested that these personality tendencies were not artifacts of laboratory settings.

A possible explanation for these personal tendencies was offered, "[s]cientists suspect that small inherited predispositions are either enhanced or suppressed by experience, and computer models show that tiny discrepancies at the start can become enormous over time, through feedback loopings of positive reinforcement". These computer models would seem to have been based on assumptions that minimized the routinely self-evident lack of environmental effect on personality. From some of the animal examples to the human realm - including monozygotic twins and also the limited behavioral import of adoption - the empirical basis for "positive reinforcement" certainly does not seem to be "enormous".

From a transcendental perspective these personalities could largely be artifacts of previous lives' experiences, experiences which could have spanned different species. Amongst some Indonesian people and also some tribes in western Amazonia there are beliefs that certain animals deserve special consideration because they can embody ancestral souls [Columbia, p.2874]. In general from a transcendental perspective, an individual's innate personality could reflect substantial contributions from previous lives. Such contributions could help explain the surprising range of personalities. Thus a personality found in any species might then represent an overlay of transcendentally acquired particular tendencies upon the general species as well as gender-specific tendencies presumed to be established by DNA. Such particular personality tendencies would not be carved in stone of course, but like the tendencies of some individuals to become alcoholics, they can pose significant challenges.

◆ ◆ ◆

An interesting and moving chronicle of surprising animal behaviors can be found in Jennifer S. Holland's *Unlikely Friendships* [Holland]. Holland's beautifully illustrated book related 47 stories of cross-species friendships. A number of the stories involved household pets including dogs. Three of the dog stories involved one "mother[ing] a baby squirrel, another parad[ing] around with chicks on his back, [and] a third buddy[ing] up with an elephant" [p.xii]. Some of these friendships appeared to defy evolutionary logic.

One story was set in the Elephant Sanctuary of Hohenwald, Tennessee and involved a female elephant named Tarra and a female dog named Bella [Holland, p.42-45]. Without precedent or apparent prompting they formed a friendship that had them eating, drinking, and sleeping together. In fact they "rarely parted". At one point the dog Bella became seriously ill and had to be treated indoors. Tarra appeared to hold a very concerned vigil outside the treatment house. After "many days" the dog recovered and they were reunited. Subsequently:

> Tarra caressed Bella with her trunk and trumpeted, stamping her feet. Bella, all dog, wiggled her whole body in excitement, tongue and tail in a nonstop wag as she rolled on the ground.

And, in a most remarkable moment, Tarra lifted one immense foot into the air and carefully rubbed the belly of her friend.

One biologist, Joyce Poole, got a chance to see the animals together and thought it was "delightful" but in the words of the author, felt it wasn't "all that surprising". Poole was quoted offering some comments about the very social ways of elephants and that "[t]hey not only adopt one another's young, they even mourn their dead". Poole's empirical perspective might make the dog-elephant friendship not "all that surprising", but one could argue that from an evolutionary perspective it appears to be (as would be the elephants' mourning behavior too).

Another interesting friendship story involved a golden retriever and a koi ("large, multi-colored goldfish") [Holland, p.50-53]. The nine year old dog Chino was not particularly interested in interacting with other dogs but showed a keen interest in watching his owner's backyard pond. He would "stretch out at the pond's edge on the warm rocks, watching as the fish circled and descended and rose up to feed." A subsequent move by Chino's owners to a new home left Chino with a new pond and a fine perch. This new pond was home to only two of the previous koi, though. At this point, perhaps aided by fewer distractions, the pond-watching dog made a friend with one of the fish, a large koi called Falstaff. Subsequently, upon being let out of the house Chino would go straight to the pond and look for Falstaff and that fish "would come right over." Their interactions involved:

> meet[ing] at the edge of the pond, and Chino would lean or lie down and put his nose in the water. They'd touch noses or Falstaff would nibble Chino's front paws.

At the pond Chino "would lie flat on his belly for a half hour or more … completely captivated by his water-bound pal."

One of the most striking friendships observed occurred between a wild leopard and a cow in India [pp. 68-71]. Reports of a leopard's nightly visitations to a cow brought some personnel from the Forest Department in the hope that the leopard could be captured and taken elsewhere. One of the forestry personnel was Rohit Vyas, a wildlife conservationist. What he and others observed was:

> [t]he cat returned to the area nightly, often many times a night, but not as a predator sniffling out a warm meal. Instead, she came to be embraced. She approached the cow tentatively, rubbed her head against the cow's head, then settled against her body. The cow would lick the cat, starting with her head and neck, cleaning whatever she could reach as the cat wriggled in apparent delight. If the cow was asleep when the leopard arrived, the visitor would gently awaken her with a nuzzle to the leg before lying down and pressing close. Other cattle stood nearby, but the leopard ignored them. The chosen cow seemed pleased to give the leopard her nightly bath. For almost two months the leopard showed up around eight in the evening and cuddled with cow until the first hint of sunrise.

Eventually the leopard stopped coming. The conservationist Vyas offered an explanation involving perhaps a motherless leopard inadvertently eliciting the mothering instincts of the cow, but he also added that:

> This relationship was unimaginable. We were all spellbound by it. Who would have expected a carnivore and hunter like a leopard to show love and affection towards its prey?

Another striking friendship was observed in the wild between a lioness and a baby oryx (an antelope) [Holland, pp.82-85]. Their relationship drew quite a bit of attention from the local people. Perhaps in the wake of it a conservationist and social anthropologist, Saba Douglas-Hamilton observed the two animals for more than two weeks. For some reason the young lioness adopted the very young oryx, in Saba's words "as if it were her cub." They "walked the land side by side and slept together, one an extension of the other." The lioness' friendship, though, could not satisfy the oryx's growing hunger and conversely the lioness' commitment led it to give up hunting. Outside experts were of no help and efforts to feed the increasingly hungry pair failed. Eventually the weakened oryx was killed by another lion. The lioness then returned to hunting but in the coming months was reported to have "adopted oryxes five more times - all for brief periods - before she herself disappeared from the area".

A final friendship considered here took place between a young 600 pound hippopotamus and a 130-year-old Aldabra tortoise and their friendship became well known [Holland, pp.190-193]. The hippo, Owen, had been rescued after he became lost from his pod in the wake of the December 2004 tsunami. After being transported to Haller Park Wildlife Sanctuary in Mombasa, Kenya Owen managed to strike up a supportive relationship with the old tortoise named Mzee. As reported by the Haller Park's manager, Paula Kahumbu:

> [Owen] began copying Mzee's feeding behaviors, chewing on the same grasses. He'd ignore other hippos bellowing elsewhere in the park, and he was most active during the day, which is the opposite of typical hippo behavior but in line with tortoise preferences. The two followed each other around, wallowed together in the pond, and slept side by side, meaty torso against timeworn shell. Owen became protective of his reptile companion and affectionate towards him, licking Mzee's face as the tortoise rested his head on Owen's belly.

While some of the general bonding may have been consistent with some instinctive parental and offspring behaviors, the underlying sustained drive for connection between such different animals is simply amazing.

Additionally, there was apparently quite a bit of communication happening between the two. Holland wrote that:

[s]cientists have been most fascinated with how the two animals developed their own physical and verbal language. With gentle nips and nudges to feet or tails, they told each other when to move and in which direction. They sounded off, back and forth, with deep rumbling sounds not typical of either animal. "What strikes me is how sophisticated their mutual communication system became," says animal behaviorist Barbara King. "It's a dynamic dance between two species with no preset program on how to deal with each other. And it can't just be instinct, because one was shaping its behavior to the other."

That acknowledgment of mystery was certainly appropriate.

◆ ◆ ◆

A transcendental hypothesis could offer an additional dimension for explaining such unusual behaviors and also for the surprising range of personalities found among animals. One basic point is that a possible transcendental dynamic would entail a generic transcending element - a soul. Such souls might then form surprising bonds, perhaps even across substantial gaps in species (and presumably facilitated by non-threatening settings). In general when evolutionary logic runs aground a transcendental perspective could offer some traction. In some rare cases like that of the gorilla Ebobo this alternative explanation might be obvious. The enormous resistance to considering reincarnation, though, appears to be piled on top of a resistance to acknowledging that animals even have personalities. Science has its rigid boundaries but outsiders are free to contemplate their own understandings.

Chapter 4

Family Mysteries

As geneticists scramble around in search of the elusive DNA origins of a number of our particulars, it is worth considering other challenges to the materialist's vision. This chapter will consider some challenges found with adoption; some behavioral genetics findings in the political realm; and also a surprising experimental result from epigenetics research. These challenges involve questions about families and parents.

The opening discussion here concerns some difficulties associated with the adoption of children. Following that discussion there is an example from the literature of possible cases of reincarnation that deals with abortion. If the reader has particular sensitivities to either of these topics then they might consider skipping ahead to the following section entitled "More Behavioral Genetics".

An apparent challenge to the current scientific understanding can be found in the process of raising adopted children. This challenge is the common occurrence of adoptee grief for a lost connection to birth parents and it appears to be overwhelmingly accepted. In adoptee and author Sherrie Eldridge's *Twenty Things Adopted Kids Wish Their Adoptive Parents Knew* this pretty much filled the book and was behind the "twenty things" [Eldridge]. A psychologist and a psychiatrist were quoted from the book *Being Adopted: The Lifelong Search for Self*, "unlike other losses we have come to expect in a lifetime, such as death and divorce. Adoption [grief] is more pervasive, less socially recognized, and more profound" [Eldridge, p.5].

Eldridge also quoted an open adoption practitioner and child welfare supervisor, James Gritter, who explained in his book *The Spirit of Open Adoption*:

> We must be careful not to sanitize, sentimentalize, or even glamorize the pain of adoption; it really is miserable stuff, and it is intensely personal. It is interior. The pain of adoption is not something that happens to a person; it is the person. Because the pain is so primal, it is virtually impossible to describe [Eldridge, p.7].

Some adoptee quotes provided included "it feels like a part of me is missing" [p.7] and "I have spent my whole life roaming and never felt stable" [p.8].

In a less grief-oriented presentation, the book *Raising Adopted Children* by (non-adoptee) Lois Ruskai Melina described that adoptive parents "often expect their children to need some time to adjust to a new family and to grieve for their birth parents or foster parents. But they may be surprised to find the children grieving for these losses years after the move" [Melina, p.147]. Continuing Melina wrote that:

> as Brodzinsky and his colleagues point out in *Being Adopted*, children who were adopted as infants usually "do not express the shock, deep depression, uncontrollable crying, or intense rage that are commonly part of acute or traumatic loss." Instead they may be withdrawn, distracted, confused, "clingy", or have occasional bouts of sadness or anger [p.147].

A relevant example appeared outside the adoption literature in the magazine *Sports Illustrated* as the writer Rick Reilly reported on experiences with his adopted daughter [Reilly]. The daughter had been born to an unwed Korean young woman and subsequently adopted by the author and his wife at 4 months of age. As a child his daughter "thought constantly about her birth mother". As a result the author, his wife, and their 11 year old adopted daughter went to Seoul to try to get to see the birth mother. After some effort and delays a short meeting with the birth mother was realized. At it the very tense birth mother did not make eye contact with her biological daughter. After a minimal exchange consisting of the daughter asking her prepared questions, the birth mother's interpreter suggested it was time to leave. The birth mother at this time broke out of control and sobbing heavily embraced her biological daughter. It seemed that the birth mother "wouldn't let [the daughter] go". After this very emotional meeting the 11 year old daughter was "beaming" and commented "it feels like it fixed a little hole in my heart".

The third and final question that the adoptee had asked her birth mother prior to the latter's emotional release was "when you had me, did you get to hold me?" The birth mother's answer was "no". The emotional release of the birth mother was not surprising. She must have been very conscious of her pregnancy and for evolution-consistent reasons was very likely to have had strong concerns about her daughter even after she was adopted [Juno]. The separation must have been a big ordeal for the birth mother (even in her subsequently married-with-children state).

On the other hand how did the adopted daughter end up with such a strong connection to someone she had never met? What is responsible for such adoption grief? Further, even if like some other adoptees they had met when she was an infant how could this bond have survived? The under-appreciated phenomenon of childhood amnesia somehow erases the memories we have from the first three or four years of our lives (this topic will be returned to). As a personal example, I have been repeatedly told about significant happenings around me as an infant prior to a move at about age 4. I can't recall any of it and thus am unable to generate significant feelings about those events.

The related topic of attachment has been studied in infants. In the text *Understanding Children's Development* by Peter K. Smith *et al* it was suggested that at around 6 months an infant can start to display signs of attachment. Based on work by John Bowlby and a student of his, J. W. Anderson, Smith *et al* wrote that:

> [t]he infant preferentially orientates to and signals at one or more discriminated persons. This marks the beginning of attachment. The infant is more likely to smile at the mother or important caregivers, for example, or to be comforted by them if distressed. Exactly when this occurs depends on the measures used, but it is commonly observed at around 5-7 months of age [Smith, p.73].

From this behavioral perspective then the brain development of an infant, combined with her/his personal experiences, allows for displays of attachment after about 6 months. Even putting aside childhood amnesia, though, this accepted 6 month milestone would not offer an explanation for the grief of adoptees who had been separated much earlier, though.

A more subtle and conceivably relevant point was also made in *Understanding Children's Development* with regard to an infant's recognition of voices. It appears that a fetus can become familiar with the voice of the mother and this connection is reflected in the ability of newborns to distinguish the voice of their mother versus that of another female. Perhaps not surprisingly one study found that "2-day-old newborns preferred the sound of their mother's voice filtered to sound as it would have [been] in the womb" over that of the natural voice of their mother. Could this voice identification reflect a significant attachment present at birth that subsequently in the case of adoptees could contribute to a feeling of grief for a lost connection to the birth mother?

Going back to Sherrie Eldridge's *Twenty Things Adopted Kids Wish Their Adoptive Parents Knew*, in it there was an effort to explain adoption grief in terms of the *in utero* experience. Eldridge's explanation utilized the book *The Secret Life of the Unborn Child* by Dr. Thomas Verny and John Kelly. Eldridge thereby suggested that:

A key concept to remember is that your child's perception about adoption began not at birth, not on adoption day, but during the first nine months of life in the womb of his or her mother. This is where your child's core personality was mysteriously woven together [Eldridge, p.15].

A mother's attitude to her developing fetus was cited as critical to its psychological development. Eldridge quoted Dr. Verny as saying, "What a woman thinks of her [in utero] child makes such an important difference" [p.16]. Further, it was suggested that the change of parents between the in utero experience and post-adoption, and possibly compounded by a poor attitude of the birth mother, engendered the subsequent adoptee grief. Again even neglecting childhood amnesia, though, this explanation appears to have problems. Are the differences in personalities between monozygotic twins - or more generally the large spread commonly found amongst siblings - due to the differential attitudes directed towards them by their expectant mothers? How could an expectant's mother attitude - unlike gross unhealthy behavior such as drinking - shape a fetus' psychological development and also possibly effect bonding? Also how much bonding is possible for a fetal brain from a neuroscience perspective (beyond the aforementioned apparent voice recognition)?

Furthermore, in modern societies many infants spend considerable time with unrelated but nurturing adults (usually women). From Eldridge's perspective why wouldn't these children subsequently experience some kind of daycare-separation grief? In fact a distributed-mothering relationship appears to be something that our species appears to be innately comfortable with. In a discussion about the book by primatologist Sarah Blaffer Hrdy, Mothering and Others: The Evolutionary Origins of Mutual Understanding, Hrdy had suggested that the evolutionary development of this shared-mothering relationship was unique among our great ape cousins and fundamental to some of our cooperative social tendencies [Angier 2009]. The human mother-sharing observations included:

> [a]mong the Efe foragers of Central Africa, babies spend 60 percent of their daylight hours being toted around by somebody other than their mother. In 87 percent of foraging societies, mothers sometimes suckle each other's children, another remarkable display of social trust.

Another explanation of adoption grief was provided by Lois Ruskai Melina in *Raising Adopted Children*. That grief was suggested to come as a result of being socialized in a society that "tells him he [her she] has lost people whose relationship to him [her] is a valued one" [Melina, p.147]. But could an abstraction like this really have much impact - emotional or otherwise - on children? As children grow up they become more involved with and motivated by abstractions, in particular ones centered on competition and status. But it is difficult to see, though, how the abstraction of a "valued relationship" could engender a significant impact on a child or even an adult. Real grief seems to have its origins in the loss of actual relationships and not in abstract or remote developments. Do people grieve over exposure to tragic stories in the news?

Additionally, if this socialization hypothesis were true then adoption grief should occur more often in cases where the issue of adoption was frequently discussed and/or it was physically apparent. As Sherrie Eldridge pointed out in the past this issue was minimally talked about and that would seem to have provided little traction for the abstraction of a lost relationship. In fact in the book *Stories of Adoption* by Eric Blau there were adult adoptees who didn't know they had been adopted until their adulthood, including one man who found this out at age 48 [Blau].

Furthering possible doubts about these adoption grief explanations, is the fact it isn't generally experienced. Sherrie Eldridge cited a thirty-something year old man who upon being offered the opportunity to find his birth parents had no interest and said "I've always felt okay about being adopted, and my parents are my parents. I don't feel any big need to know any more than I do about my past, and I'm not aware of any adoption issues I need to deal with" [Eldridge, p.7]. In another adoption book, *Be My Baby*, by Gail Kinn this was also reflected in the experiences of some adult adoptees.

So what could be the basis of adoption grief? Could fetal experience have produced such grief? A socialized or conditioned basis appears to be too weak for something that can show up strongly in childhood. Additionally, would adoptive parents be inclined to pity their children over their adopted status?

Continuing with adoption grief, in the aforementioned sports article, "Heart and Seoul", there was another side to the adoption grief topic presented. Beyond the daughter's case, the case of an adopted professional athlete was also considered. That athlete had also been born in Korea and raised in the United States. As a child, though, this athlete-to-be displayed no interest in his biological parents despite having an adopted brother who did. Eventually as an adult he became interested in his biological parents via interactions with other adoptees at a Korean Heritage Camp. This could simply be socialization-born interest, though, and does not appear to be a strong demonstration of something innate. Adults can certainly be swayed socially. In fact the praise given in Sherrie Eldridge's book was heavily from psychologists and/or therapists and the underlying emphasis on adoption grief with the potential for therapy-based treatment could prove attractive to adult adoptees (and therapists), even if they hadn't previously distinguished significant psychological pain associated with their adoptions. As adults we naturally want to feel good and will try many routes as is evident for example with the many existing forms of therapy and self-help protocols.

I suggest then that some childhood cases raise significant questions, as they provide evidence of a surprising difficulty experienced by some adoptees. It would be good to have some numbers on this phenomenon. Perhaps what percentage of adoptees regularly as children expressed an interest in their biological parents and what percentage pursued finding those parents (although currently the pursuit is much easier with the internet). Even in her less grief-oriented book, Lois Ruskai Melina acknowledged that "[i]t is not unusual for an adoptee to become obsessed with the search - spending all her energy on it and talking about nothing but finding her birth parents" [p.202].

One possible explanation from a transcendental perspective is that an incarnating being tends to be drawn to specific parents and sometimes this attraction is personal. From an examination of traditional African reincarnation beliefs it was suggested that "the ancestor is only reincarnated in his own family" [Head and Cranston, p.173]. Likewise amongst the Australian aborigines it has been reported that they believe their babies are the "reincarnation of deceased ancestors" [Columbia, p.2874]. Reincarnation researcher Jim Tucker pointed out that among cases suggestive of reincarnation, "[t]o hear of children crying for years for their family to take them to their previous parents until the family finally relents is not unusual" [Tucker 2005, p.116]. Many of those investigated cases appeared to involve memories of previous human lives, lives which often ended violently and unexpectedly.

But of more particular interest to a possible adoption grief explanation here, were two cases from Tucker's *Life Before Life* in which young children displayed strong regret for not getting the parents they had previously wanted. These cases were unusual in that the apparent memories were almost exclusively from the discarnate realm, not the previous life. Both claimed to have been *in utero* in earlier failed pregnancies of other women. In one case the failure was a miscarriage and the other an abortion.

In the miscarriage case a boy named Bobby from North Carolina had "frequently talked about wanting to live with his cousins" [Tucker 2005, pp.164-168]. Bobby "repeatedly said that he belonged with his cousins" and referred to the oldest boy amongst his cousins as his "big brother". These statements didn't arouse much interest with Bobby's parents who figured it to reflect a passing preference for his cousins' larger family. This changed when after a bath as a four and a half year old, Bobby first queried his mother on her memories of his being inside her and then his younger brother Donald being inside her, and then secondly on Donald and him together being inside her. When his mother corrected him about Donald in the last scenario, Tucker reported that Bobby added "they were in her tummy at the same time but did not get born". After a subsequent correction by his mother, Bobby responded that "he and Donald had been in Aunt Susan's tummy at the same time, rather than his mother's, and asked why Aunt Susan did not give birth to them."

At this point Bobby became incensed at his two and a half year old brother Donald and screamed:

> Donald, it is all your fault. I told you I wanted to get born real bad, and you didn't want to. How did you take me out of there, Donald? Why didn't you want to get born? Tell me how you did it. Tell me how you took me out of there.

After restraining Bobby his mother added his brother Donald didn't understand what he was yelling about. Bobby insisted he did and then Donald removed his pacifier and yelled back "No! I wanted Daddy". Bobby then responded back yelling "I didn't want Daddy, I wanted Uncle Ron!"

After a calming period Bobby went on to tell his mother that after that failed pregnancy he tried to be born again to Aunt Susan but his cousin Rebecca was there. Bobby said "I wanted to be in there, and she wouldn't let me. I tried to kick her out, but it didn't work. She got to be born, and I didn't." Bobby went on to say, "I sure did have to work hard to get here, Mom."

The Uncle Ron here was the brother of Bobby's father. His wife Susan had had a miscarriage involving male twins seven years before Bobby was born. This miscarriage had occurred after the birth of their only son (the boy whom Bobby had called his big brother). The miscarriage had happened thirty-three weeks into the pregnancy and a subsequent examination showed that there had been a vulnerable umbilical cord which the doctors thought may have been pinched closed when a twin rolled over on it. Bobby had also made some remarkable and accurate comments with regards to his parents' wedding (during which his mother was pregnant with him) and of his own difficult birth.

The point of note here, though, was the apparent preference to be born with specific parents and that this circumstance was analogous to an adoption in that the child ended up with different parents. Bobby's younger brother Donald also offered that single utterance about his own previous (and realized) preference. In Bobby's case, his preference was apparently a pretty significant while he was young.

In the second case from Tucker's *Life Before Life* a young girl in Florida appeared to identify a woman who previously had been pregnant with her and this pregnancy had ended in an abortion. For the girl, Kendra, this perception was very significant [Tucker 2005, pp.114-116]. At age 4 and a half years old Kendra went to her first swimming lesson. Her coach was named Ginger and Kendra upon arriving "immediately jumped into Ginger's lap and acted very lovingly towards her. When Ginger had to cancel a lesson three weeks later, Kendra sobbed uncontrollably." This was the beginning of some very unusual behavior by Kendra.

Upon getting back to her swimming lessons, Kendra started talking about her instructor Ginger frequently. Within a few weeks Kendra described to her mother an abortion and said that Ginger had had one and that "I'm the baby that was in her tummy." Kendra's mother later found out from Ginger that nine years before Kendra was born, Ginger had been unmarried and sick and had had an abortion. The child Kendra then proceeded to go through tremendous anguish, feeling that she would die because Ginger had not delivered her. After visiting a therapist and going through a ceremony to confer a sense that she had been "born" to Ginger, Kendra's fear of death appeared to subside.

Although Ginger was frequently unfriendly towards Kendra, Kendra's ongoing intense desire to be with Ginger eventually led Kendra's mother and Ginger to work out an arrangement whereby Kendra spent three nights a week at Ginger's home. Later after a disagreement between the women, Ginger decided to stop seeing Kendra. Kendra subsequently did not talk for four and a half months. The child "showed no interest in activities, ate little, and slept a lot." After this period she met with Ginger for a couple of hours and spoke again for the first time in telling "Ginger that she loved her." After the meeting Ginger started calling Kendra again, but Kendra - apparently consoled - started to return to a more normal life and didn't want to go to Ginger's house anymore.

These events were deeply disturbing for Kendra's mother who was not only concerned about her daughter's wellbeing but also the apparent evidence for reincarnation. As a conservative Christian "she felt that she was committing a sin by merely buying a book on reincarnation during Kendra's troubles." Kendra had never been alone with Ginger at the swimming lessons and had no apparent basis for her strong reaction to Ginger. Kendra's mother eventually decided, "that Kendra's spirit had been looking for another body after Ginger's abortion, but she did not accept the idea that reincarnation is a process that normally occurs."

In the context of a possible transcendental basis for adoption grief, Kendra's experience is consistent with the belief that an incarnating being can be attracted to a particular parent (or parents) and also suggests that this attraction can continue and possibly re-surface in a later incarnation. From this perspective, Kendra's close encounter as a child with Ginger appeared to trigger a psyche-avalanche associated with their previous connection. A potential parallel with an adopted child experiencing adoption grief is that this thwarted earlier desire to be with a parent (or parents) can continue and cause some distress. A difference, though, in Kendra and Bobby's circumstances is that from a transcendental perspective they could also have experienced a personal draw to their subsequent parents.

Although, some traditional beliefs in metempsychosis insist that the process is bound to families, perhaps this hypothesis was more common in and consistent with small closed populations. Within the possible reincarnation cases investigated by Jim Tucker and Ian Stevenson there were cases in which the selection of parents did not appear to based on a close personal connections. Some of the more striking examples were cases in which a child claimed to remember the life of a soldier in an invading army. Stevenson investigated a number of cases involving Burmese boys claiming to have been members of the Japanese army in World War II. The behavioral correlates to the claimed transcendental connection were that these boys appeared to standout because of their Japanese and rough soldierly behaviors. In one case a boy claimed to have died in the spring of 1945 at the city of Rangoon's (Burma) zoo - fearing capture he and some fellow retreating soldiers had committed suicide - and continued to hang around there until "he saw his (present father) and followed him home" [Stevenson, p.31]. His father confirmed that he had been to Rangoon's zoo before the boy's birth and then had returned the 400 kilometers to his home unaware of anything unusual. The boy was born in 1972.

The topic of adoption will be returned to in the next chapter.

More Behavioral Genetics

A thorough-going example of behavioral genetics was found in the paper "Are Political Orientations Genetically Transmitted?" by John R. Alford, Carolyn L. Funk, and John R. Hibbling published in the May 2005 issue of the *American Political Science Review* [Alford *et al*]. Of particular interest here this offered a look at the degree of agreement on positions amongst monozygotic twins. Alford *et al*'s abstract succinctly stated:

> We test the possibility that political attitudes and behaviors are the result of both environmental and genetic factors. Employing standard methodological approaches in behavioral genetics - specifically, comparisons of the differential correlations of the attitudes of monozygotic twins and dizygotic twins - we analyze data drawn from a large sample of twins in the United States, supplemented with findings from twins in Australia. The results indicate that genetics plays an important role in shaping political attitudes and

ideologies but a more modest role in forming party identification.

The latter point about party identification is consistent with some previous findings from behavioral genetics studies that some attitudes (including religious identification) appear to be significantly influenced by parental socialization. Note that the monozygotic and the dizygotic twins in the studies were 18 or older and that the overwhelming majority of the pairs had been raised together.

This political study offered some relevant numbers for opinions on social and political issues. Each American twin studied was presented with a list of 28 topics including "pacifism", "death penalty", "nuclear power", and "abortion" and asked for one of three responses - "agree", "uncertain", or "disagree" (which could in turn be numerically coded as 1, 2, or 3). Alford, Funk, and Hibbling were mostly interested in the implications for the political tendencies of liberal and conservative which turn out to be a common dichotomy around the globe. Of particular interest here, though, is the degree of agreement or correlation found amongst the monozygotic or identical twin pairs.

The issue of pacifism had a (polychoric) correlation of 0.34 amongst the monozygotic American twin pairs, and a correlation of 0.15 for their fellow dizygotic twins (where a correlation factor of 1.0 reflected perfect agreement, 0.0 coin-flipping like random agreement, and -1.0 reflected perfect disagreement). There were 2,576 monozygotic twin pairs and 1,686 dizygotic twin pairs responding on this issue. These correlation values were then used to obtain an estimate of 0.38 for the inferred DNA contribution (or heritability) to an individual's position on pacifism. The formula for the estimate was two times the difference in the monozygotic and dizygotic correlation values, $2 * (0.34 - 0.15) = 0.38$. The value of 0.34 for the monozygotic twin correlation is noteworthy. Like many of the 28 issues considered in the study this would seem likely to be a relatively static position. I would be inclined to think that most adults have a fixed position on pacifism over much of their adult life. Yet the correlation amongst the study's monozygotic twins on this issue was only 0.34.

Together with the other 27 opinion items in Alford *et al*'s American twin data set, the overall mean for monozygotic correlation was 0.47 and the corresponding estimated mean for item heritability was 0.32. The corresponding mean of the items' shared environment contribution was 0.16 and this value contributed to inflating the mean of the monozygotic twin correlations and simultaneously reducing the heritability estimate. A number of the opinion items appeared to have a significant parental socialization (or shared environmental) contribution which tended to push any two offspring towards agreement, regardless of their innate dispositions. The issue abortion, for example, had a shared environment contribution estimate of 0.39.

Articles like this 2005 article have apparently been followed up by many others and a sub-field of political science, termed genopolitics, has formed. An October 2013 article in the *New York Times*, "Are Our Political Beliefs Encoded in our DNA?", offered a survey of opinions on its findings and significance [Edsall]. In this article even one of the most critical perspectives offered on genopolitics really came off as a marginal rebuttal. In it Evan Charney of Duke University claimed:

> It is not our claim that genes do not affect behavior. Of course they do. It is, rather, that there are not genes, whether one gene or 10,000, that "predispose" to being a 21st century American liberal or conservative, or to voting in an American political election, and that these behaviors are not "heritable". A gene (whether 1 to 10,000) can only play a causal role because "the environment" - cells, tissues, organisms - uses genes to create proteins ... DNA is one resource among others used by cells. Development is not the running of a preexisting genetic program.

Note here that Charney was loose in stating that "DNA is one resource among others used by cells" and in a scientific sense should have stated something like, "DNA is the blueprint or design resource used by cells". He had also e-mailed in a comment that with "genome wide complex trait analysis"-based searches "in many cases [their findings are] statistically insignificant". Putting his two comments together we get "of course" "genes" affect behaviors, even if the corresponding genetic searches come up empty. There is a tremendous amount of momentum towards accepting that DNA created us and this momentum tends to play out in the scientific world as well as with laypeople's understandings.

From a transcendental perspective the apparent heritability of political orientations could simply reflect a tendency to be drawn towards similar-minded birth parents, coupled with a tendency towards behavioral continuity. Thus, in a simple example an individual with strong feelings about the death penalty might then be drawn towards a reincarnation with parents possessing similar feelings. The apparent heritability connection would then be loose, though, because the continuity-based rebirth draw towards parents would likely be averaged across other positions and behavioral tendencies, and also possibly be coupled with a draw based on past personal connections.

An Epigenetic Oddity

Finally, some noteworthy experiments have taken place in the epigenetics field. As reported on in Eric J. Nestler's "Hidden Switches in the Mind" *Scientific American* 2011 article, it appears that normal mice can be environmentally conditioned to become relatively "anxious and fearful" as adults through being raised by a "fearful, passive mother" and that this conditioning takes place "at least in part, through epigenetic modification" [Nestler]. That conditioning effect involving some epigenetic modification of the DNA's chromatin also tends to make those conditioned mice "nervous and neglectful caretakers". Thus, it appears that epigenetic modifications (or markings on the chromatin) are involved in long term behavioral conditioning of mice and moreover that that conditioning can have effects on multiple generations. By contributing to the production of female mice who grow up to be poor mothers, it appears that epigenetic effects are capable of setting up a generational cycle (i.e., poor mothers produce epigenetically-influenced female offspring who in turn become poor mother themselves, who then produce ...). Note, though, that this inheritance-like effect does not involve the direct transmission of behavioral tendencies. Analogous phenomena may also have been apparent (to both laypeople and professionals) with regards to the abusive treatment of offspring.

On the other hand, Nestler pointed out that "[s]everal groups have found that chronically stressed rodents give birth to offspring that are particularly sensitive to stress". One example given was:

> Isabelle Mansuy of the University of Zurich and her colleagues subjected mouse pups to maternal separation during their first two weeks of life and found that, in adulthood, the male offspring exhibit signs of depression. When these males are bred with normal mice, the resulting offspring also show similar depression-like behavior as adults, even though they were not subject to stress during their upbringing. This transmission of vulnerability to stress correlates with altered levels of DNA methylation of several specific genes in both sperm and brain.

This result is suggestive of an inheritance effect, an effect that would seem to be taking place via the transmission to the offspring of the depression-contributing, epigenetic modifications (involving DNA methylation marks along the chromatin) found in their depressed dads. This could generally be very significant as it could imply that some inheritance - perhaps including a portion associated with the missing heritability problem - is in fact taking place via the epigenome and not directly via the DNA code itself. If some of the epigenetic behavioral-conditioning dynamics could be shown to have a direct inheritance aspect as well, then some of an individual's basic behavioral tendencies - such as their inclination towards getting stressed out, or depressed, or becoming addicted to a particular drug - might have been established via the specifics of their conception-delivered epigenome.

But as followup on such efforts, Nestler and colleagues decided to more explicitly check the possible epigenetic inheritance connection. They repeated the original experiment and also found a "profound increase in [offspring's] susceptibility to depression". Then as a check they replaced the original mating step with an artificial mating using sperm extracted from the depressed mice dads. If epigenetic markers were the vehicle for the apparent transmission of susceptibility to depression then, Nestler *et al* had reasoned, that those markings would have had to have to reached the sperm cells. But in this artificial union scenario it was found that the resulting offspring "were almost completely normal: they showed only slight indications of the withdrawn behavior and anxiety evinced by their fathers".

Nestler went on to put a qualification on this apparent negative finding in that perhaps the relevant epigenetic marking had been stripped off in the *in vitro* fertilization process. Furthermore, Nestler went on to write that in sum their experimental findings:

> suggest that the females that had physically mated with intimidated males treated their pups differently than females that had mated with normal males - or that never met the fathers of their pups. Consequently, the offspring's depression may have stemmed from an early behavioral experience and not from a direct epigenetic inheritance carried through sperm or egg.

This comment is worth a pause. If this behavioral effect was in fact happening, think of the enormous possible implications for mating males' psyche-states - including of course transient ones - and also for the *in vitro* fertilization business! On a similar vein a noteworthy Op-Ed article in the *New York Times*, entitled "Why Fathers Really Matter", contemplated the possible "game-changing and terrifying" implications of epigenetic experiments [Shulevitz].

Furthermore, in conjunction with Nestler's tentative conclusions he went on to point out that, "[o]f course we now know that an individual's genes play the dominant role in determining physiology and function". But if the presumed genetic basis does not pan out in the genome searches; the epigenetic experiments don't support an epigenetic alternative vehicle; and speculative environmental explanations don't find much traction - then science had better look elsewhere for answers to their inheritance mysteries.

A possible transcendental take on these epigenetic experimental results is simply more of the same - an incarnating being tends to be drawn to their future parents. The characteristics of those parents - potentially reflected in their DNA or its epigenetic marking state - are part of that draw and thus you end up with apparent inheritance effects. Relatively aggressive parents would then tend to draw incarnating beings who themselves were inclined to be relatively aggressive. The strong apparent inheritance effects associated with being an alcoholic ("more than 50 percent of the overall risk for alcoholism is attributable to inherited factors"), for example, could then reflect such a transcendental dynamic and not the elusive DNA specifics [Nurenburger et al]. Additionally, the earlier considered case of the Einstein Syndrome in which remarkably nerd-inclined children were born almost exclusively to nerd or nerd-connected parents would then reflect a very potent rebirth route.

Furthermore, the particularly surprising Nestler experimental sequence - the apparent inheritance of depression-prone tendencies with regular mating and then none with artificial mating - is approachable transcendentally via a description given in the *Tibetan Book of the Dead* [Freemantle]. In that text it is repeatedly described that the tendency is to be drawn to your parents in "union". The negative result obtained by Nester *et al* was obtained by using the sperm extracted from a sacrificed mouse dad. That could then be hypothesized as a markedly different union scenario, in particular with the behavioral-standout mating participant - the chronically-depressed dad - having been sacrificed. If this seems too absurd reflect back on the environmental alternative left to Nestler which entailed a female mouse somehow committing to poor motherhood due to the bummed-out state of her mouse stud.

I add a follow-up comment on the mouse experiments. These experiments, as noted in a comment by Nestler, are inherently brutal. I am suggesting here some potential significance in the associated findings but I do not want add motivation for additional similar experiments. Perhaps epigenetic researchers can devise relevant experiments which are more humane.

◆ ◆ ◆

I end this chapter on an interesting possible individual case of reincarnation with a family connection from outside the reincarnation literature. This case also provides an example of the kind of long term continuity that a transcendental process might entail. The case came from the experience of Cornell University's nutritional scientist T. Colin Campbell. Campbell had spent most of the latter part of his career researching the under-appreciated possible health benefits of a plant-based diet [NYT diet]. In 1985 while on sabbatical in Oxford, England, he came upon the work of a London surgeon named George Macilwain who had practiced and researched in the early 1800's. After some genealogical research Campbell came to the conclusion that Macilwain was his great-great uncle. Campbell later wrote:

> This discovery has been one of the more remarkable stories of my life. My wife Karen says, "If there's such a thing as reincarnation …". I agree: if ever I lived a past life, it was George Macilwain. He and I had similar careers; both of us became acutely aware of the importance of diet in disease; and both of us became vegetarian. Some of his ideas, written over 150 years ago, were so close to what I believed that I felt they could have come from my own mouth [Campbell, p.344].

The suggested transcendental connection between Campbell and Macilwain would have been along family lines and demonstrated both occupational-similarity and dietary-commitment continuity. There could have been one or more intervening human incarnations. There is no apparent basis for a personality comparison other than the inference that both individuals could endure being outsiders in the health field.

Chapter 5

Groups and Gender

An interesting May 2007, *Scientific American* article, "Prime Directive for the Last Americans", profiled the Brazilian activist Sydney Possuelo. The 67 year old Possuelo has spent his working life trying to "protect the way of life of isolated indigenous groups in the Amazon rain forest". Possuelo's conclusion as presented in the article was that a policy of avoiding any contact with such groups is best. This represents an about-face from the long standing policy of "integration" in which it was assumed that civilization was a blessing that should be shared.

Possuelo described his experiences in meeting an isolated Brazilian group:

> you must keep an eye on the folks who are there. The guys fight you with bows and arrows, they kill you, they speak up to you, they assault you. [and after contact] One year later they are slack, emaciated, bowing their heads and begging for food and money by the roadside. You break down their health, their mythical universe, their work and education system. They become outcasts, and many of them have been outcasts for 500 years.

Possuelo's concern for such people had led him to the sober conclusion of avoidance (although his description was guilty of overstatement as they obviously didn't kill Possuelo).

Of interest here is the final phrase - "many of them have been outcasts for 500 years". There appears to be plenty of truth to this conclusion and truth going well beyond the Amazonian context. Why are there such significant differences between the priorities and lifestyles of groups long after there appear to have been ample opportunities to integrate, if only on some basic life-supporting issues like education? The traditional explanations seem to largely fall into one of two camps - cultural barriers or, alternatively, pervasive bias against those groups underachieving in mainstream priorities. These two explanations - one based on internal and the other on external obstacles, respectively - have produced large resonances in the political sphere as well. From the first perspective, the economist and researcher Thomas Sowell has documented in books such as *Race and Culture: a World View* the "reality, persistence, and consequences of cultural differences" between groups. These differences appear to stubbornly persist across diverse settings.

From the materialist or scientific view an explanation is limited by the understanding that genetic blueprint- or DNA-wise, groups appear unlikely to differ significantly and thus you have to look to some combination of the cultural or differential social/institutional treatment explanations. Sowell's analyses suggested that differential social treatment and in particular biases against outsiders, are very common so that group differences are likely primarily based on cultural factors (Sowell's work has also chronicled the unintentional problems associated with corrective preferential policies). A possible sticking point with a cultural understanding, though, is the limited environmental impacts associated with adoptions. Cultures may play a big part in driving the different (average) behaviors found amongst groups, but what is it that produces those cultures? On a related point, how effective are cross-cultural adoptions at influencing adoptees' cultural inclinations? The origins of cultural differences perhaps pose their own mysteries.

The Industrial Revolution

A thorough and thought-provoking look at some relevant group-differential terrain can be found in Gregory Clark's *A Farewell to Alms: A Brief Economic History of the World* [Clark]. This novel look at human economic history had at its core three questions. They were:

> Why did the Malthusian Trap persist for so long? Why did the initial escape from that trap in the Industrial Revolution occur on one tiny island, England, in 1800? Why was there the consequent Great Divergence [p.3]?

The Malthusian Trap refers to the population growth-stymied state of all economies prior to 1800. Clark crunched the economic status of societies down to the metric of average income per person, a figure based on the amount of basic living stuffs they could purchase with a single day's earnings. Before 1800 it appears that no society had experienced long term increases in this income metric. Thereafter, starting with England some have sustained very rapid increases in average income. Clark's broad historical data analysis produced a startling caption for an opening figure that began with "World economic history in one picture" [p.2] (interestingly that figure - and the later "Real income per person in England" plot [p.195] - were similar in form to the famous "hockey stick" plot of the Northern hemisphere's rising temperatures over the last millennium).

The above reference to the "Great Divergence" refers to the post-Industrial Revolution division between societies in which per capita income has rocketed up and other societies in which per capita income has actually fallen. As Clark commented "there walk the earth now both the richest people who ever lived and the poorest" [p.3]. In 2007 when *A Farewell to Alms* was written the ratio between the incomes of high and low earning societies was about 50 to 1.

Clark suggested that in the Malthusian Trap "the economy of humans ... turns out to be just the *natural* economy of all animal

species, with the same kinds of factors determining the living
conditions of animals and humans" [p.5]. Clark expounded:

> In the Malthusian economy before 1800 economic
> policy was turned on its head: vice now was virtue then,
> and virtue vice. Those scourges of failed modern states -
> war, violence, disorder, harvest failures, collapsed
> public infrastructures, bad sanitation - were the friends
> of mankind before 1800. They reduced population
> pressures and increased material living standards. In
> contrast policies beloved of the World Bank and the
> United Nations today - peace, stability, order, public
> health, transfers to the poor - were the enemies of
> prosperity. They generated the population growth that
> impoverishes societies [p.5].

Thus the horrible sanitation found in preindustrial Europe - where
"filthy people ... squatted happily above their own feces, stored in
basement cesspits" - produced a beneficial higher mortality rate
than for example found in the sanitation-minded and crowded
Japan.

A Farewell to Alms went to great lengths to show that globally
per capita income didn't improve prior to 1800. And then came the
Industrial Revolution in which as characterized in a quote of
Donald McCloskey:

> In the eighty years or so after 1780 the population of
> Britain nearly tripled, the towns of Liverpool and
> Manchester became gigantic cities, the average income
> of the populations more than doubled, the share of
> farming fell from just under half to just under one-fifth
> of the nation's output, and the making of textiles and
> iron moved into the steam-driven factories. So strange
> were these events that before they happened they were
> not anticipated, and while they were happening they
> were not comprehended [p.230].

Clark argued that requisite to these developments appeared to have been changes in the priorities and behaviors of the British people during the long prologue to that revolution. He commented that during this lead-up "[i]nterest rates fell, murder rates declined, work hours increased, the taste for violence declined, and numeracy and literacy spread even to the lower reaches of society" [p.8]. Although seemingly independent of the concurrent revolutionary manufacturing developments, England's population and fertility during this revolution rose sharply and thus limited the per capita income gains. Subsequent reductions in fertility, though, then allowed for big rises in per capita income. Such roll backs in fertility were also found in other industrialized societies and largely predated the arrival of modern contraceptive methods [p.294].

One of the remarkable points made in the book was the existence of stubborn differences between worker performances in different societies. After Britain's industrial revolution was well underway, other societies seemingly should have been able to replicate and perhaps exceed the success of the British. This appeared to have been particularly true amongst groups within the British Empire. Clark claimed that by 1900 "cities such as Alexandria in Egypt, Bombay in India, and Shanghai in China were all in terms of transport costs, capital markets, and institutional structures, fully integrated into the British economy" [p.12]. Apparently stymieing these follow-up revolutions in such societies was poor worker performance.

One example considered in detail by Clark was India and the cotton industry. The textile industry had been the Industrial Revolution's flagship and in particular it had "accounted for more than half of all productivity" advances during the period [p.233]. With the basic processing of raw cotton into cloth, 18 man-hours of labor had been required to transform a pound of cotton in the 1760's. One hundred years later, technical developments had reduced this figure down to 1.5 man-hours [p.234]. The textile technology utilized was surprisingly simple and was also generally available via exports from British engineering firms. There was a large open international textile market and presumably local markets everywhere. Early on the British had dominated the world market for cotton cloth but given that their biggest production cost was unskilled labor (62% as of 1911 [p.338]) the potential in low wage areas appeared to have been excellent. From an 1893 assessment:

> India enjoys a great advantage over England, for the advantage which England possessed in regard to skilled labor most certainly does not apply as in former years ... with the marvelously perfect and self-acting machinery of today no special skill is required on the part of the attendant. The machinery itself supplies the intelligence; all that is required from the workman is attention in "following up" the machinery, such as piercing up broken ends [of thread], doffing and other simple details, which are performed by the native Indian cotton factory operative almost as well as by his European brethren, and at far less cost to the spinner [p.337].

Clark in fact felt that by 1850 or so poor countries like India, "with their huge advantages in labor cost, should have taken over the cotton textile industry, driving out the British from the unprotected markets" [p.337]. This reasoning seemed sound at the time and thus by 1895 there were 55 cotton mills in Bombay, India alone. The cost of labor was much lower there, a figure for 1910 showed that Indian cotton mill wages were 16% of their British counterparts [p.338].

The real problem with regards to the reasoning given in the previous 1893 assessment was that the "Indian cotton factory operative" didn't come close to performing as well as their "European brethen" and thus the big promise of the Indian wage advantage was not realized. The poor work quality of Indian mill workers effectively undid their low labor costs. Gregory Clark went to great lengths in *A Farewell to Alms* attempting to show that none of the institutional or more generally external factors appeared to explain these differences. Of the 55 cotton mills in Bombay in 1895, 27 of them had British managers [p.356]. Some plants tried reducing the number of employees and but then had to raise wages. The bottom line over many years, at many plants, using different labor schemes was the politically incorrect reality that "Bombay mill workers seemingly worked at low intensity and in a slapdash manner, so that employers were forced to assign many workers per machine to achieve full output from their invested capital" [p.360]. More generally, "the problem of persistent inefficiency in labor use in poor countries ... was the main barrier to the spread of the technologies of the Industrial Revolution" [pp.345-346].

The intellectual question that Clark sees at the heart of the Great Divergence is - why couldn't some groups get more committed to the tasks that were requisite to the economic potential of the Industrial Revolution? (A parallel question not considered here was how did that revolution result in the crucial demographic transition?) The same differentials in worker commitments have continued and apparently been a big factor in the Great Divergence. Clark suggested that these behavioral differences were a natural selection-based. He suggested that those successful in the modern era are likely "the descendants of the strivers of the preindustrial world" [p.376]. Clark chronicled possible mechanisms including the higher fertility rates of the economically successful in England from 1250-1800. From some data for the beginning of the seventeenth century, for example it was claimed that the "richest men had twice as many surviving children at death as the poorest". Gregory Clark suggested that with this dynamic "the attributes that would ensure [England's] later economic dynamism - patience, hard work, ingenuity, innovativeness, education - were thus spreading biologically throughout the population" [p.8]. Clark did not see this in bigger terms and in fact his thoughtful conclusion argued against a number of superficial economic-success-produces-happiness lines of reasoning (the preface and introduction also touched on this). Additionally, the Industrial Revolution obviously has not helped with regards to humanity's sustainability challenges. Nonetheless, that revolution poses significant historical questions.

In considering some other explanations, I can think of one somewhat analogous scenario involving group differentials which has an environmental or conditioning basis. Sometimes in informal adult recreational gatherings there can seem to be two groups present. Those comfortable and skilled with the activity and others who are clumsy and lost at a basic level. This can seem particularly strange when these differences appear to contradict fitness levels. These differences can sometimes coincide with national origins. My sense is that with such scenarios they reflect previous exposure - probably as a kid - to the recreational activity. Thus, if you grew up playing catch or kicking a soccer ball then you are probably pretty competent at that activity, but if you did not then you are very likely a klutz at it. It is difficult to think that something like that, though, would explain the manufacturing worker performance differences considered here. As noted in the 1893 British assessment, these are not complicated skills and it is hard to imagine children anywhere doing something analogous to build up a head start to carrying them out as adults.

Another possibility would be that the Indian workers were significantly less healthy than their British counterparts. This would have been very poor health indeed, though, given the miserable sanitation of nineteenth century England. Such differences might also have been visible.

Clark's suggested genetic explanation in *A Farewell to Alms* raised additional questions and drew some attention. First, was the claimed pre-Industrial Revolution, class-based reproductive dynamic really unique to England? In a review for the online journal *Evolutionary Psychology* an anthropologist, Laura Betzig, claimed it was not [Betzig]. Higher reproductive success for the rich appears to have been the norm everywhere in the historical written records. Betzig perhaps went a bit overboard in giving many examples of the colossal fertilities of emperors, but she did address and rebut Clark's particular assessment of why the dynamic officially failed in China. She claimed that there the legitimate children were a small minority and that the claimed numbers of consorts for Chinese emperors in a number of dynasties reached into the hundreds if not thousands.

In his chronicle on the historical decline of violence, *The Better Angels of Our Nature*, Steven Pinker added some additional challenges to Clark's reasoning including the perhaps questionable, "when institutions change, a nation can vault itself to spectacular rates of economic growth in the absence of a recent history of selection for middle class values, such as postwar Japan and post-communist China" [Pinker 2011, p.621]. Clark, though, had offered plenty of historical evidence that institutional measures have not worked. Additionally, one might argue that Japan and China have had histories containing very disciplined traditions that could have provided an analogous basis or springboard for Clark's suggested selection dynamic, or simply provided an effective cultural training ground. Altogether though, Betzig's and Pinker's analyses, plus the very limited amount of time available for the suggested natural selection dynamic, do not appear to be supportive of Clark's biological explanation for England's role in the Industrial Revolution. His extensive environmental analyses, though, at the least highlights some interesting group mysteries surrounding this watershed event.

On a somewhat parallel historical footing, Pinker's *The Better Angels of Our Nature* had to address the possibility of a biological/genetic basis contributing to the apparent rollback in violence amongst humanity that was the central message of that book. Although Pinker did acknowledge recent findings suggesting that the dynamics occurring in the human genome have been higher than expected (believed to be consistent with more active evolutionary selection pressure), and that the apparent selection dynamics varied amongst populations - he also pointed out that the particular genetic studies including those involving the so called Warrior Gene - suggested to be related to aggressive behavior - have not been convincing [pp.613-614, pp.619-622]. Pinker of course stands by the implications of behavioral genetics studies of aggression which have suggested that that this tendency has a significant heritable basis (roughly half), but he went on to conclude that:

> while recent biological evolution may, in theory, have tweaked our inclinations toward violence and nonviolence, we have no good evidence that it actually has [p.621].

This non-genetic conclusion is the norm amongst those considering group differences and of course is analogous to the rebut of Clark's genetic hypothesis.

Moreover, the non-genetic conclusions are consistent with the unfolding big picture. The many inferences drawn from behavioral genetic studies notwithstanding, if DNA assessments are not showing a basis to differentiate the innate behavioral inclinations of individuals, then DNA analyses would certainly seem unlikely to shed light on the much smaller average differences found between groups. The missing heritability problem casts a large shadow.

◆ ◆ ◆

As with the earlier considered hypothesis by Alford *et al* on the DNA basis for political views, you certainly can't fault Gregory Clark for considering an evolutionary/biological basis for the group differences relevant to their participation in the Industrial Revolution. Academically, Clark appeared to have opted out of political correctness in favor of scientific correctness. Flawed as his DNA explanation could well be, though, the alternative institutional explanations apparently do not add up, as he chronicled. Furthermore, you certainly can't fault Clark for doing extraordinary data collecting and analysis. Underlying general questions with regards to group cultural differences seem to persist in the economic domain, as well as elsewhere.

A possible transcendental explanation of group differences and dynamics is an extension of the previously considered process. A being would tend to be reborn locally within her/his group and bring along some of their previous tendencies and preferences. In this way a group - as the sum of such individuals - could have its own particular behavioral inclinations or agendas. Additionally this process could be dynamic as the members in a group invest more or less energy into different pursuits. Such a phenomenon could in turn be coupled with (or complementary to) the evolved default behavioral tendencies (with their presumed DNA basis) that are common amongst all humans.

From this perspective, continuity across death could then have played a significant part in the transformation of behaviors in England that eventually led to the Industrial Revolution. If there was an increasing tendency amongst the English towards behaviors conducive to an industrial way of life, then some of their kids could have been born bearing some of the relevant inclinations. They already would have had a leg up, so to speak. Such a process would be similar to that previously considered as an explanation for the surprising Flynn Effect and also with the very focused Einstein syndrome.

International Adoptees' Cultural Needs

Another group behavioral mystery is associated with adoption and it is the apparent need of some international adoptees for their birth country's culture. (As previously noted if a reader is particularly sensitive to the adoption issue they might consider skipping ahead to the following section.) This phenomenon is born out from both the adoptive parents' and adoptees' experiences. In Gail Kinn's *Be My Baby*, one adult international adoptee suggested giving other international adoptees as much of their native culture as you can. This individual had gone through an enormous self-initiated push into the culture of his biological parents. This not uncommon drive has led to the existence of culture camps where parents of international adoptees can provide brief periods of native cultural exposure for their adopted kids.

The question for consideration here is, is this drive something innate and surprising, or is it something superficial and conditioned? There is no scientific reason to think that culture is something passed on via the DNA. Scientifically, an individual's culture - like their language - should be acquired through their environmental exposure. On the other hand, perhaps if a child were born in Korea (to Korean parents) and then raised in Saudi Arabia, their unique appearance combined with their innate self-consciousness might drive them to plunge into Korean culture for some relief. But in a diverse setting like that quite commonly found in a country like America, how much sense would this make?

A relevant *New York Times Magazine* article entitled "Why a Generation of Adoptees is Returning to South Korea" by an adoptive parent Maggie Jones, considered the recent phenomenon of adult adoptees returning to live in their birth country, South Korea [Jones]. The author was sympathetic to the frustrations of these South Korean adoptees as she and her husband had adopted a Guatemalan child. The adult adoptees interviewed discussed their own displeasure with being an adoptee in America as well as their draws back to South Korea. The article also described some related efforts by adult international adoptees - some from South Korea and elsewhere too - to work against international adoptions. Although the article conveyed acknowledgements from adult adoptees of the sincere, well-intentioned efforts they had received while growing up in America, there was an underlying dissatisfaction with their experience.

In the comments following Jones' article there was a strong clash of interpretations. The second most recommended comment (or Readers' Picks) read:

> I'm sickened by how [an adoptee] treated her parents. What a victim complex she has. And how delusional to think that the place she spent her first couple of months is somehow her 'real home'. The whole problem with the thinking of so many people in this article is summed up in the sentence:

"But she was yet another child who, through no choice of their own, was leaving her biological family, her country and her culture behind."

She's an infant. She doesn't yet have a culture. The whole premise that a person is deeply and inherently connected to a country's culture just because of their skin color and because they spent a little time in the country before they could speak is absurd.

Although blunt that comment is certainly accurate in a scientific sense. We are not supposed to born with a culture. On a somewhat of a similar vein, another top pick read:

I think these people are extremely ungrateful to their adopted parents, extended families and the country where they were raised. They are lucky people loved them. There is nothing magical about birth families. Just because you are biologically connected to another mother, another father and their family groups means nothing. The people who love, feed, clothe you, burp you as a baby, nurse your wounds and illnesses as a child, teach you how to get along in the world, are your "real" family. It is sad that these people get to the age of 30 or so and have no clue what a family is.

Another strong rebuttal to the dissatisfied adoptees' positions. On the other hand another Readers' Picks comment read:

I'm a Korean adoptee. I lived in Seoul for about 5 years. I've been back in the States for almost 5 years. Like many in this article, I feel like I never fully fit in - not American enough, not Korean enough. My parents are wonderful people, loving and caring. Despite my parents' love, despite my shiny, happy childhood, as an adult now I live with a pain that I can't fully explain. It's deep. And it's awful.

And the comments saying adoptees should be grateful, that biological families aren't always wonderful, that being raised in an orphanage would be worse than being adopted into a loving American family -- to you, I say, you don't understand. And maybe you don't need to understand. But I wish you would show more compassion.

Thousands of international adoptees live in pain every day. Your judgement invalidates the truth of their pain, which I know from experience is very, very real. Your compassion could help them heal.

Adoptees are so rarely allowed to grieve our losses - loss of family, language, culture, history, identity. We are expected to be grateful, to count our blessings. I love my parents, deeply. Also I also need to grieve for all that is lost.

Also present amongst the comments, though, were those of other adult Korean adoptees who apparently were comfortable with, and appreciative of, their adoptions. So where does the truth lie here - with the frustrations of some adult international adoptees or with the modern intellectual understanding? For those disagreeing with the critical adult adoptees, it is worth noting that their efforts are anything but casual. Adults have to be seriously motivated to move to a place where they have "no friends, no employment and no fluency in the language".

Related material had also been considered in an earlier *New York Times* article entitled, "Adopted From Korea and in Search of Identity" by Ron Nixon [Nixon]. That article offered some findings from a large transracial study of adoption, in particular looking at:

the first generation of children adopted from South Korea, [it] found that 78 percent of those who responded had considered themselves to be white or wanted to be white when they were children. Sixty percent indicated their racial identity had become important by the time they were in middle school, and, as adults, nearly 61 percent said they had traveled to Korea both to learn more about the culture and to find their birth parents.

One adoptee described had shunned her Korean heritage until an incident in her thirties when she was overwhelmed with grief. As suggested in the previous chapter, seemingly inexplicable demonstrations of strong emotional bonds appear to be much more mysterious when they occur amongst children, but with adults such demonstrations are also intellectually intriguing (and of course significant to those individuals).

One interpretation based on the transcendental perspective of the frustration experienced by some international adoptees, is that an incarnating being not only tends to be drawn to specific parents, but as suggested above also tends to be reborn locally. In Jim Tucker's *Return to Life* he pointed out that amongst cases suggestive of reincarnation, "[t]he previous person was from the same country as the child in over ninety percent of our cases, often having lived fairly closely" [Tucker 2015, p.202]. Historically these two aspects of the process could have tended to overlap since most people didn't move far in a lifetime (and even with migratory animals they are locked into a few locations). If the process is usually local then a new born child could well have lived previously in the vicinity and thus had some exposure to the local culture. Thus in the Korean example, an internationally adopted Korean child may face the dual challenge of ending up with different parents and a different culture than the ones that they had chosen or been drawn to. In this understanding, someone born to Korean parents in Korea would tend to be in some surprising innate way, Korean. For some internationally adopted Koreans this might then surface as a significant problem. One corollary of this hypothesis is that Korean children conceived of and born in the United States should be less likely to experience an apparent need for Korean culture. Another corollary is that an individual who stands out from their group could have spent their previous human life in a different group.

These points about the origins of an international adoptee's interest in the culture of their biological parents might be too subtle for a formal study. On the other hand, though, the points might be of interest to someone involved with international adoption who has puzzled over this phenomenon. The Brazilian scenario opening this chapter is a good one to end the discussion about groups on. How much of the behavioral differences between the indigenous and modern Brazilians is inborn or innate? If by some mix-up two newborns were unknowingly swapped between the two groups, how would these two individuals do in their respective societies? Would they fit in so that in the end no one suspected that something was awry? Or would they tend to be like the proverbial fish out of water?

Gender Mysteries

Another collection of mysteries for science is found with unexpected gender-related inclinations. Innate homosexual inclinations pose an obvious contradiction to evolutionary reasoning. Evolutionary/biological explanations of this phenomenon are not convincing.

A return to the male monozygotic twin example considered in the first chapter highlights the mysterious nature of the homosexual phenomena [Collins, pp.204-205]. Although it certainly appears to be an inborn or innate trait, again the likelihood of concurrence on male exclusive homosexuality amongst monozygotic twins is only 20 to 30 percent. Somehow it seems that when homosexuality occurs within a male monozygotic twin pair it usually occurs amongst only one of them. Also among males it appears that the likelihood of being born with a homosexual inclination increases by about 30 percent for each older brother. The discussion in Collins' *The Language of Life* alluded to possible explanations involving cumulative biological changes in the mother due to her previous male pregnancies, although it also noted a lack of relevant support.

The challenge for science with regards to male exclusive homosexuality would then seem to be to identify a loose DNA basis and also a means to ramp up the resulting gay likelihood by 30 percent per older brother. Alternatively, from a transcendental perspective there is no reason to expect anything of DNA (beyond Y chromosomes). Being gay just happens to reflect a soul's history, perhaps involving a previous gender change. The 20 to 30 percent monozygotic twin gay-agreement could reflect their previous relative closeness, with perhaps some of the complementary 70 to 80 percent of discordant twins having been drawn together based on a previous heterosexual relationship. The 30 percent per older brother dynamic could reflect a secondary rebirth draw for such souls. The more boys present - male energy if you will - then the greater the draw to that family.

More surprising when considered from the materialist perspective appears to be the transgender phenomenon. It seems that in the last several years media coverage has opened to the fact that some individuals appear to strongly identify as the opposite gender. Readers can find a number of articles discussing this unexpected and challenging situation, for example the *New York Time Magazine*'s "What's So Bad About a Boy Who Wants to Wear a Dress?" [Padawer]. What kind of scientific explanation appears plausible in the case of people who spend their entire lives wishing they were the opposite sex? Additionally, one study noted that amongst the subset that have undergone sex-change efforts (or transitioned) many "knew they had been born into the wrong gender from childhood" [Landau]? Such an explanation would seem to require some kind of mutation in the DNA which resulted in an individual whose brain then felt committed to identifying with the opposite gender. It is worth recalling that behind the scenes here, of course, are just programmed molecular interactions where the perceived entities including self and free will are simply illusions. This is difficult to envision.

From the above cited *New York Times Magazine* here are a few excerpts. At 3 years of age:

> he insisted on wearing gowns even after preschool dress-up time ended. He pretended to have long hair and drew pictures of girls with elaborate gowns and flowing tresses. By age 4, he sometimes sobbed when he saw himself in the mirror wearing pants, saying he felt ugly.

Such behaviors can pose a challenge for parents. As one father put it, "I didn't know how to be the father of a girl inside a boy's body". And of course such a behavioral/identity orientation can impose a significant strain on a transgender individual living amidst their society's gender norms.

One self-assessment by an eight year old in Andrew Solomon's *Far From the Tree* contained:

> I'm a girl and I have a penis. They thought I was a boy until I was six. I dressed like a girl. I said, 'I'm a girl.' They didn't understand for the longest time [Solomon 2012, p.604].

And then looking ahead the same 8 year old (after commenting on possible solutions to their penis challenge):

> [w]hen I'm a mommy I'll adopt my babies, but I'll have boobies to feed them and I'll wear a bra, dresses, skirts, and high-heeled shoes [pp.605-606].

As a biological backdrop here the reader might try juxtaposing these comments with the prominnet biologist Ernst Mayr's opinion that "[t]here is not a single Why? question in biology that can be answered adequately without a consideration of evolution" [Mayr, p.xiii]

Such gender mysteries encourage consideration of environmentally-based explanations. In the above cited *Times Magazine* transgender article one authority was cited in suggesting transgender environmental influences involving "overprotective mothers, emotionally absent fathers or mothers who are hostile toward men". Reading this it is not hard to flash back to critical commentaries on environmentalism such as Steven Pinker's in *How the Mind Works*:

> [f]or most of this century [20th], guilty mothers have endured inane theories blaming them for every dysfunction or difference in their children (mixed messages cause schizophrenia, coldness causes autism, domineering causes homosexuality, lack of boundaries causes anorexia, insufficient "motherese" causes language disorders) [p.48].

Pinker of course presumes that there are largely DNA-based explanations.

Another glimpse of a possible scientific explanation for the transgender phenomena was given in Solomon's *Far From the Tree*. It was as follows:

> Heino Meyer-Bahlburg, a professor of psychology at Columbia University who specializes in gender variance, has described numerous possible biological mechanisms, and said that as many as four hundred rare genes and epigenetic phenomena may be involved, genes associated not with hormone regulation, but with personality formation. 'The view we have of the brain now is like those wonderful pictures of earth that the first astronauts took from the moon,' said Norman Spack, associate professor of pediatrics at Harvard University and leading endocrinologist in the field [p.607].

How seriously should we take this? Unless you are "swept along by metaphors, as are readers [and perhaps authors] of popular science" [Sheldrake, p.163], you realize DNA simply provides elemental blueprints for protein molecules and in some cases regulation of associated processes. The extrapolation of that elemental dynamic to a thorough reversal of an individual's gender identification appears to be an extraordinary act of faith in DNA. The above epigenetic commentary appears to be even more speculative. The neighboring challenge here for any DNA explanation is of course the lack of concurrence on male exclusive homosexuality amongst monozygotic twins.

The possible interpretation offered by the transcendental perspective is the obvious one - an individual's gender is the opposite one from its previous incarnation and identity/behavioral continuity established the current dilemma. What ultimately may not be a big deal - a soul simply changing the gender of its incarnation - can produce significant challenges and lessons in the embodied world.

Chapter 6

The Religion and Science Context

The heritability problem considered in this book challenges science's materialist vision and it also opens a door to some potential objective support for a religious understanding of life. An appropriate context for that discussion is the charged but mostly static Religion-versus-Science divide. This chapter thus focuses on some relevant aspects of that charged contemporary divide. The chapter opens by critiquing some of the characteristics of modern science and its following. Coverage in the *New York Times* is considered as exemplary of this. Then it critically considers the lack of effort on the part of the religious to try to make some objective sense of their beliefs. In an extended discussion the confused contemporary state of the religion of Buddhism is examined. Finally, this chapter considers some noteworthy items that fall between the realms of science and religion.

SCIENCE

From a modern secular, and certainly intellectually-oriented perspective, a meaningful dialogue between religions and science does not appear to be possible. From this perspective, science tends to be an essentially idealized vehicle for truth, and religions on the other hand are simply superstitious traditions from the prescientific era. From the friendlier side of the secular camp you can get some acknowledgements of the potential well-being benefits associated with religious involvement, although invariably this in the context of it being delusion-based help and one might then wonder about the well-being import in the context of a delusional labeling. And of course from a science-anchored perspective none of the transcendental business which has been discussed here - or any dualistic alternative - can even be considered.

I think of the educated secular position as being thoroughly embodied by the coverage of the *New York Times*. Their coverage of issues relevant to the Religion-versus-Science divide is skewed strongly towards the scientific position. This skewed coverage might be argued as not too far from the norm, though, in the sense that direct questioning of science's materialist position is unusual amongst any secular media that I am aware of. What appears to distinguish the *Times'* coverage is their overt veneration of science.

I will start into my coverage of science with a qualification on the use of the word "science" herein. By that word I mean fundamental academic science which is centered on the topics of biology and physics. The perspective of modern biology is of course of a material-only understanding of life and this purview appears to have won out in the intellectual sphere and thereby marginalized any serious consideration of a non-material or spirit-aspect of life. Perhaps now in a more focused sense, neuroscience embodies this material-only or spirit-nixing perspective. Modern physics on the hand, appears to have in part become sort of an intellectual surrogate for religion. It offers grand mysteries - sometimes across staggering scales - with regards to the specific details of the material universe and its history. Perhaps equally important it carries enormous intellectual prestige. From this twin perspective, modern biology has dismissed the traditional spirit-based understandings of life, whilst physics has unleashed a torrent of intellectual energy directed towards investigating the details of fundamental material processes. In a basic sense it seems that this contemporary scientific influence has pushed to replace a traditional appreciation for "amen" with one for "brilliant!".

To complete my qualifications here on the topic of science, I want to clearly state that the practical side of science is not being criticized here. If people want to investigate some pressing and/or practical matters and that entails what might generally be labeled scientific efforts then that is certainly commendable (although obviously the details of any particular investigation may be flawed), and also it rarely conflicts with religious positions. One prominent environmental example has been the study of the dynamics of Earth's climate which of course has involved scientific investigations, but on the other hand it has been a very marginal topic within academic science. On that point interested readers might try identifying physics departments which during the last 30 years have been home to more research on the Earth's climate than those of other planets.

I think it can be a worthwhile learning experience looking up the research topics considered in some biology and physics departments. The terminology encountered can be intimidating and confusing, but you can pick up some of the gist of their agendas. In general you may find some potentially practical work, more likely within biology departments, but the majority is simply furthering basic scientific knowledge - and of course careers and reputations. On a relatively practical and lively topic like Conservation Biology, the *Petersen's Guide to Graduate Programs* listed 26 American programs across by 2 and half pages [Petersen's]. On a more academic topic like Cell Biology there were 228 programs listed across 17 and a half pages. One revealing search is to try to find applied physics departments (although one physicist told me that even there practical work is eschewed). Another is to see if you can find a biology faculty member (at a secular school) who in any way questions the material-only understanding of life.

♦ ♦ ♦

I get started here in this consideration of the science end of Religion-versus-Science with a quote from Albert Einstein on whether he was religious:

> Yes, you can call it ["religious"]. Try and penetrate with our limited means the secrets of nature and you will find that, behind all the discernible laws and connections there remains something subtle, intangible and inexplicable. Veneration for this force beyond anything that we can comprehend is my religion. To that extent, I am, in fact religious [Isaacson, pp.384-385].

This quote certainly sounds religion-friendly and other similar quotes can be found. There also are a number of quotes in which Einstein was critical of atheists. On a related note, a purported Einstein quote was used frequently by Western Buddhists to provide some modern intellectual credibility for Buddhism.

But moving on, the specifics of Einstein's positions were not consistent with real religions. At one point he had said, "I am a determinist. I do not believe in free will." [Isaacson, p.387]. In another that, "[h]uman beings in their thinking, feeling, and acting are not free but are as causally bound as the stars in their motions" [p.391]. Finally, Einstein had offered "no" on the belief in immortality question. Einstein's relevant positions appeared to reflect the perspective of a profoundly intellectual person who was apparently deeply appreciative and moved by the depths of the universe's material mysteries, but rejected any traditional religious beliefs. One could say that such deep appreciation of, and commitment to, scientific mysteries - or other topics for that matter - might be deemed "religious", but this is not what real religions entail.

Along these lines in the relatively critical Einstein biography, *The Private Lives of Albert Einstein*, Roger Highfield and Paul Carter suggested that the young Einstein simply transitioned from an initial reverence for God to a subsequent reverence for science and a resulting rejection of religion at about age 12 [Highfield and Carter, p.17]. His initial reverence for God has been described as including "compos[ing] his own hymns for the glorification of God, which he sang to himself as he walked home from school" [Isaacson, p.16]. But at age 12 his plunge into reading popular science had led him to believe "that the stories from the Bible could not be true, and [he] swung to the opposite extreme of fervent doubt" [Highfield and Carter, p.17]. Shortly after this transition he had written:

> Out yonder there was this huge world, which exists independently of us human beings and which stands before us like a great, eternal riddle, at least partly accessible to our inspection and thinking. The contemplation of this world beckoned like a liberation, and I soon noticed that many a man whom I had learned to esteem and to admire had found inner freedom and security in devoted occupation with it [p.17].

Highfield and Carter went on to frankly suggest that Einstein "who had found neither security nor freedom in human relationships, and whose attempt to find them in religion had failed, would seek them now in science" [p.17].

Perhaps his initial reverence for God was simply innate and his transition towards the intellectual pursuits of science formed a strongly conflicting attraction. Young Einstein was very bright (and an excellent student) and could likely sense that he had significant potential in science, but the authority and prestige associated with science conflicted with his simpler religious instincts. He then could have simply rejected the latter which might be a common response for intellectuals. Additionally a strong focus on intellectual pursuits tends to reduce awareness and interests elsewhere, certainly with non-intellectual topics like religion.

◆ ◆ ◆

Next I move on to some samples of popular perspectives on science. The following two quotes were taken from the comments following a science article published in the *New York Times*. The first quote:

> Who needs religion when reality is so amazing.

And the second:

> I commend the *New York Times* for giving this story front page status. It's exactly where it belongs.
>
> Congratulations to the scientists who never receive enough credit for their extraordinary work and great contributions they make to the human race in this amazing field!
>
> I can remember that it wasn't that long ago that <noun_1> were still considered just a theory. Our growth in the field of <noun_2> has been amazing the last few decades. I look forward to more of this news, and as a taxpayer, am willing to spend whatever it takes to give these gifted people all the tools they need for their work. Lets start by making sure Congress provides the funding needed for the <noun_3>! It would be a travesty to have it canceled.

The second commenter later added in a response to another comment, "[t]he more problems we have on Earth, the MORE important this stuff becomes." These comments were in response to the article, "Astronomers Find Biggest Black Holes Yet", by Dennis Overbye and the respective deleted nouns in the second comment were "Black Holes", "Astronomy", and the "James Webb Space Telescope" [Overbye 2011]. Needless to say one might argue about the significance of black hole research along with the gist of these comments. This might simply be done by noting that these are lifeless entities of which the nearest reported on was an estimated 331 million light years away.

The above article appeared to have been substantially based on a graduate student's e-mailed comments and it also was somewhat hyped as appears to be common for science coverage in the *New York Times*. It did, though, offer an outside investigator's perspective in which Martin Rees of Cambridge University characterized the work as simply "an incremental step". Further, the two comments above were respectively the number 1 and 2 "Readers' Picks" comments and the second commenter had earned a special designation as not needing review prior to publication. For additional perspective here, I can report that on a number of occasions my comments that questioned scientific materialism have not been displayed.

◆ ◆ ◆

Some more detailed, and perhaps sober, perspectives on black hole research can be found in the August 2012 *Scientific American* article by Caleb Scharf, "The Benevolence of Black Holes" [Scharf]. In the article Scharf laid out some evidence of the apparent dynamic existing between the structure of a galaxy and its central black hole, and in particular for the resulting potential to support the development of life. Scharf pointed out that:

> The connection between the phenomenon of life and the size and activity of supermassive black holes is quite simple. A fertile and temperate galactic zone is far more likely to occur in the type of galaxy that contains a modestly large, regularly nibbling, black hole rather than a voracious but long since spent monster.

After cringing past the larger why-is-the-universe-amenable-to-life (or anthropic) question, the article went on to report that our Milky Way galaxy happens to be "smack dab in the [life-habitable] sweet spot of supermassive black hole activity". Furthermore, Scharf went on to write that:

> [t]he entire chain of events leading to you and me
> would be different or even nonexistent without the
> coevolution of galaxies with supermassive black holes
> and the extraordinary [matter and energy] regulation
> they perform.

Thus many of the details of the universe's galaxies and stars appear to have been dependent on black hole dynamics and this can be viewed as adding to the already staggeringly long evolution- and conception-based odds against the existence of "you and me".

Scharf concluded his article with a reverential paragraph:

> This fertile corner of the cosmos has been governed by
> all that has gone on around it, including the behavior of
> the black hole at our galactic center. The very places
> that have sealed themselves away from the rest of the
> universe have served as one of the most influential
> forces shaping it. We owe so much to them.

This appears to reflect science's reverential search for our material origins and as such perhaps overlaps with Einstein's religion. A further expression of that reverential perspective was also given in the opening sentences of the article. There Scharf had written:

> [o]ur existence in this place, this microscopic corner of
> the cosmos, is fleeting. With utter disregard for our
> wants and needs, nature plays out its grand acts on
> scales of space and time that are truly hard to grasp.
> Perhaps all that we can look to for real solace is our
> endless capacity to ask questions and seek answers
> about the place we find ourselves in.

This veneration of the intellect is arguably fundamental to what might be called the Religion of Science, and together with science's rigid presumption of materialism, has likely made conflict between science and religions inevitable. I think this worship of the intellect has also likely worked against the general appeal of science, although it certainly appears to have generated some support among its followers.

◆ ◆ ◆

Further perspectives on science were present in a February 24, 2014 article in the *New York Times* entitled, "Alda Alda, Spokesman for Science" by Claudia Dreyfus [Dreyfus]. In the interview Alan Alda offered the following explanation in response to a question about how he became "so passionate about science":

> Through reading. When I was in my early 20's, I started reading every article of every issue of *Scientific American*. At the time, I'd been reading a lot about the paranormal and telepathy, and I thought Scientific American would help me know if any of that was true. There, I discovered a whole other way to think, based on evidence. And so I left my interest in spiritualism behind, in favor of critical thinking.
>
> After that, I began to read books about science avidly. Even today, it's what I mostly read.

This could well be true for a number of other followers of science who might provide similar answers (although perhaps without references to paranormal and telepathy).

Alda went on to describe his role as host of the television series, *Scientific American Frontiers*, which eventually involved "around 700" interviews with scientists. He also described his own realization that scientists needed to improve their communication skills which ultimately led him to establishing a Center for Communicating Science at the State University of New York at Stony Brook. Significantly, in response to Claudia Dreyfus' question, "[d]on't you find this [miscommunication] sad because scientists have a great story to tell?", Alda had replied:

> Every experiment is a great story. Every scientist's life is a heroic story. There's an attempt to achieve

something of value, there's the thrill of knowing the unknown against obstacles, and the ultimate outcome is a great payoff - if it can be achieved. Now, this is drama!

A fine "critical thinking" assessment of science from someone who has probably gleaned very little real understanding from his own superficial exposure. I also find it very difficult to believe that he obtained any meaningful critical takes on paranormal phenomena which are not considered by scientists or *Scientific American* (and rarely, for that matter, by skeptics).

In closing here, Dreyfus had introduced the Alda article with:

The most popular speaker at the recent meeting of the American Association for the Advancement of Science was not a scientist but one of science's most high-profile advocates: the actor and writer Alan Alda.

Apparently Alda's simple idealistic take on science has fans amongst scientists.

◆ ◆ ◆

Moving on to more of the *Times*' perspective on science I turn again to an article by their science reporter Dennis Overbye entitled, "Elevating Science, Elevating Democracy" [Overbye 2009]. In response to President Obama's 2009 Inaugural Address in which he spoke of "restor[ing] science to its rightful place", Overbye wrote about that rightful place. He got started by writing, "[t]he answer, I would argue, is On a Pedestal" but not because of "penicillin, digital computers and even the Big Bang". Overbye argued that although scientists' search for truth "has transformed the world in the last few centuries", more fundamentally it taught human values including "honesty, doubt, respect for evidence, openness, accountability and tolerance and indeed hunger for opposing points of view".

Overbye went on to describe science as "in many ways [a] utopian anarchy" and that it is "[a]rguably ... the most successful human activity of all time". He also added that it "is not [accurate] to say that life within it is always utopian" followed by a somewhat predictable reference to the pharmaceutical industries' influence. Overbye's final destination was to suggest a big political import, in particular that "[s]cience and democracy have always been twins". There appears to have been quite bit missing in Overbye's assessment. In general one might wonder where the modern tsunami of scientific cleverness has taken us. Additionally, what has science's relationship been to our unfolding sustainability crisis? In particular, how have they responded to it? Furthermore and more subtly, at what cost has science's worship of the intellect come in terms of influencing our modern psychological priorities and wellbeing?

Continuing, other than an apparent annual questioning of the lack of women and select minorities in its ranks, and also a recent (and overdue) increase in attention to problems within medical science (including of course pharmaceutical shenanigans), the *New York Times'* position has translated to minimal questioning of science in general and none of its materialist vision. I think there is room to debate about Overbye's assessment of the values taught by science. From my own experiences I would suggest that "indeed hunger for opposing points of views" would have been more accurately stated as "indeed contempt for opposing points of views". Additionally, perhaps Overbye might consider at some point embodying some of his idealism by starting to question his revered topic of physics. More generally the *Times'* might suggest to their Opinion section people that they start questioning their own science-promoting agenda, perhaps by balancing a typical ode to science (and religion-bashing) piece like Lawrence M. Krauss' "A [Higgs] Blip That Speaks of Our Place in the Universe" (July 9, 2012) with something critical, perhaps entitled, "A Blip That Speaks of the Priorities of Physicists".

One letter to the editor in the *Time's* did contain a critical perspective on the work of physicists, though. The critical content was perhaps inadvertent but it was nonetheless significant. The letter's publication was probably due in no small part to the authors' being professors. Nonetheless, that January 30, 2011 letter, written by the two physicists, Jay M. Pasachoff and Naomi Pasachoff, read:

> It is not only sad that such a productive atom smasher as the Tevatron in Illinois will be shut down but it may also not be wise. When, in 1993, Congress shut off funds for its superconducting supercollider being built underground in Texas, many of the newly unemployed physicists found jobs on Wall Street. Wouldn't you rather have the nation's physicists smashing protons than designing and smashing collateralized debt obligations [Pasachoff and Pasachoff]?

This is consistent with a more modest pedestal.

◆ ◆ ◆

On the Religion-versus-Science topic, the *New York Times'* position appears to further the contentious stalemate. In particular, since their position will not allow for consideration of objective support for religious (or dualistic) beliefs the topic of Religion-versus-Science has been thoroughly skewed. As one expression of this skew in the last few years they have had anthropologist T. M. Luhrmann write a number of unique Op-Ed articles on religious people and their practices [Luhrmann 2013, 3 samples]. These articles have been done in what might be described as a scientifically-correct academic fashion. In so doing they have in no way considered an objective basis for any religious beliefs and predictably the articles - and of course their religious subjects - have been heavily mocked in the readers' comments. T. M. Luhrmann appears to have completed her academic duties; the *Times* gets to score some nominal religion-friendly points; and the prevailing triumphant secular position embodied by the *Times* gets to further intellectually marginalize and mock the religious.

The larger Religion-versus-Science relevant outlet in the *New York Times*, though, I would argue has been the column, The Stone, which is described as "a forum for contemporary philosophers". To balance their prevailing scientism they apparently decided to offer some philosophical alternatives. A number of these pieces - and certainly the ones that challenged materialism and/or atheism - have been mostly mocked demonstrations of the irrelevance and obscurantism common in modern philosophy. The outcome - these easily mocked pieces are the presumed rationally-informed, academic-kosher, improvements over religious beliefs - appears to further strengthen the science-anchored position of the *Times*. It is a challenge to try to come up with any article in the *New York Times* during the 21st century that objectively challenged scientific materialism.

As a further sample of the asymmetry in the *Times'* coverage, consider that on February 14, 2014 they published an Op-Ed piece by a University of California at Berkeley mathematician, Edward Frenkel, entitled "Is the Universe a Simulation?" [Frenkel]. Apparently a serious topic amongst some academics - including the cited Oxford philosopher and a follow-up team of University of Washington physicists [web presentation] - is that we might "be in someone else's computer simulation", a simulation "based on the laws of mathematics". As is not unusual for such science contributions it ended on some solemn notes - "[t]he jury is still out on the simulation hypothesis" but even with a not guilty verdict such work "may hold the key to understanding our reality". Also, of note was the publication date, and the fact it achieved "Most Viewed" and "Most Shared on Facebook" status at the *Times* (a point of pride provided at Frenkel's website).

Of additional note here was the fact that this simulation article generated no letters. From my following of the *New York Times*, I am confident that if they had published an Op-Ed piece offering speculative support for an alternative or religious understanding of life they would have received a torrent of dismissive letters. Somewhat to their credit the *Times* probably would have scoured the torrent for some relatively polite dismissive letters to balance out the published collection. For some context here, the following day the *Times'* Nicholas Kristof published an Op-Ed piece which led to 5 letters to the editor, including some heat from academics

[Kristof]. The topic of Kristof's piece concerned the irrelevance of non-scientific, academic work.

◆ ◆ ◆

I wind down here with some general observations about the possible import of science's position of materialism. I have spent about 10 years now trying to find relevant academic people with an interest in some straightforward challenges to materialism. With the exception of some e-mail follow-up from one standout psychology professor, one probably outcast philosopher, and recently a couple of reincarnation-connected religious professors, I have completely struck out. As with my very rude interactions with potential reviewers after submitting a paper to the online medical journal Cureus, the overwhelming response from academia has been knee-jerk rejection. I would argue that the trickle down from this science-led contempt has been a lessening of the public's willingness to seriously consider alternatives to materialism (beyond perhaps speculating about some rare paranormal phenomena or hanging on to some contradictory religious beliefs). Scientism has largely prevailed in modern societies.

RELIGIONS

On the other side of this divide are traditional religions and my interest here is in considering possible objective support for their beliefs. Those beliefs I think can be divided into beliefs in a God (or gods) and also beliefs in a soul. Proving the existence of God (or gods) is apparently very difficult and perhaps inherently ambiguous. Efforts based on 'origins of the universe' or 'how did life arise given so much ambiguity in the underlying physics?' type arguments do not appear impressive and are as inherently remote from life as are the topics of modern physics. What life-significant implications would follow from success with these types of arguments? Is there any real-life - as opposed intellectual - return in telling ourselves that with our living experiences we are "creating God's experience" [Haisch, p.xii]?

Less remote are arguments with regards to the inadequacy of the evolution of life as a material-only process such as considered in Stephen C. Meyer's *Darwin's Doubt*. But what living import would follow from concluding that there must have been some external intelligence (or Intelligent Design-er) facilitating the emergence of life on Earth? Any more than with the philosophical arguments in Thomas Nagel's *Mind and Cosmos* suggesting that there must be some other ingredients in the universe to have allowed for the emergence of consciousness? Are there any useful insights that would follow from such conclusions? Does Intelligent Design in fact even challenge the robotic determinism that naturally falls out of scientific materialism? One might argue that Meyer's optimistic take on DNA's representation of biological information - including his minimization of the junk portion of DNA - further encourages a belief in genetic determinism. Additionally how could this efficient view of DNA be squared with the much larger genomes of simpler species or the obvious differences between monozygotic twins?

Moving on, I think some of the strongest evidence in support of a religious perspective is indirect. As pointed in *Born Believers* young children seem to have an innate tendency to - or simply innately possess - a belief in God [Barrett]. My own relevant experience was in having a child of about 3 years old walk into an adult conversation I was involved with and simply say, "There is a God". The child then paused and repeated this. I remember that the adult conversation I was involved with had touched on the subject of God and probably involved a questioning of the existence of God. As far as I know that 3 year old had no relevant religious background and even if he did I doubt it would have mattered. It was striking to have a young and obviously sincere child insist on the existence of God with a conviction seemingly on par with a declaration of "I need to go to the bathroom". For some additional context here I had previously observed that the same child had sometimes demonstrated phenomenal recall of past events.

Do I think that a declaration like this coming from an infant - like others reported on in *Born Believers* - is simply fall out from evolution? Absolutely not. I would argue that such evolutionary assertions reflect an extraordinary faith in evolution (and materialism). How could biology possibly get explicit declarations of unlearned concepts out of a young child? Situations like this appear to resonate with Darold Treffert's observation about prodigal behavior typically involving demonstrations of un-learned knowledge or skills, and thus are also suggestive of a transcendental connection or at least a pre-birth existence. I would also suggest that in addition to trying to find support for some religious beliefs by examining cases of near-death experiences [Alexander; Fox; Burpo; Thondup] - a phenomena which clearly can reflect elements of personal conditioning - it would also be worth considering the common occurrence of a religious perspective amongst infants.

Continuing, though, even if you acknowledge the potential religious (and non-materialist) significance of the declarations of young children, the information conveyed could be very limited as suggested in *Born Believers*. Perhaps there is an underlying entity "God" which we innately or intuitively know of (and then perhaps forget or become too embarrassed to acknowledge), but what significance to our lives would this amount to? Perhaps we have somehow intuited the underlying sort of additional ingredients suggested by Nagel or outside influence suggested by Meyers. Ultimately though, I think if science's materialist vision can be accurately extended to account for our experiences and behaviors - as presumed by science and its followers - then that would minimize or eliminate any possible living import consistent with religious beliefs.

In addition to their all-too-human tendency towards rigidity, I think the big problem facing religions in the modern world is simply their unwillingness to try to make objective sense of their beliefs. It is difficult to imagine continued large scale sincere participation in religions without such efforts. With the ongoing parade of materialist presumptions it would seem likely that people will for the most part increasingly drift away from sincere faith in religious beliefs. The one countervailing force, though, could be that the arrogance associated with science will increasingly generate substantial reactionary tendencies.

The Religion of Buddhism

I focus most of my commentary on religions here on the one that I have some familiarity with, Buddhism. I get started by taking some excerpts from an article at the website of an American Buddhist magazine *Tricycle*, "10 Misconceptions about Buddhism", by two American professors of Buddhist Studies, Robert E. Buswell, Jr. and Donald S. Lopez, Jr. [Buswell and Lopez]. The first of the misconceptions is that "All Buddhist meditate" which the authors rebutted in part with "[m]editation has traditionally been considered a monastic practice, and even then, a speciality only of certain monks".

The next three misconceptions were relatively superficial - "[t]he primary form of Buddhist meditation is mindfulness", all "Buddhists are vegetarians", and all "Buddhists are pacifists". The fifth misconception was a big one, "Buddhism is a philosophy and not a religion". In its entirety this entry read:

> Buddhism has many philosophical schools, with a sophistication equal to that of any philosophical school that developed in Europe. However, Buddhism is a religion, by any definition of that indefinable term, unless one defines religion as a belief in a creator God. The great majority of Buddhist practice over history, for both monks and laypeople, has been focused on a good rebirth in the next lifetime, whether for oneself, one's family, or for all beings in the universe.

This is arguably the central misconception about Buddhism as it is interpreted by Western Buddhists.

On a somewhat similar note the sixth misconception was, "[t]he Buddha was a human being, not a god, and the religion he founded has no place for the worship of gods". Here the entry was:

> Buddhism has an elaborate pantheon of celestial beings (devas, etymologically related to the English word "divinity") and advanced spiritual beings (bodhisattvas and buddhas), who occupy various heavens and pure lands and who respond to the prayers of the devout.

Next, on the presumed anti-religious form of Buddhism, Zen, the authors Buswell and Lopez had an entry titled, "Zen rejects conventional Buddhism. Zen masters burn statues of the Buddha, scorn the sutras [teaching of the Buddha], and regularly frequent bars and brothels". Here the entry was:

> Zen monks follow a strict set of regulations, called "pure rules," which are based on the monastic discipline imported from India. Most Zen monks have engaged in extensive study of Buddhist scriptures before beginning their training in the meditation hall. And although one of the Four Phrases of Zen is "not relying on words and letters," Zen has the largest body of written literature of any tradition within East Asian Buddhism.

The eighth misconception about Buddhism was another significant one and was entitled, "[t]he Four Noble Truths are noble." The correction offered for these "Truths" was:

> The famous phrase "Four Noble Truths" is a mistranslation. The term "noble" in Sanskrit is *aryan*, a perfectly good word meaning "noble" or "superior" that was ruined by the Nazis. Aryan is a technical term in Buddhism, referring to someone who has had a direct experience of the truth and will never be reborn as an animal, ghost, or hell being. The four truths of suffering, origin, cessation, and path are true for such enlightened beings. They are not true for us, we don't understand

that life is suffering. So the term means, the "four truths for the [spiritually] noble."

This misconception is consistent with the common Western belief that the Buddha was, if you will, a regular person and what he accomplished in his life (in particular an end to the psychological component of suffering), we - even as distracted laypeople in an increasingly distracted era - can also expect to accomplish in our lives.

The ninth misconception was also dedicated to Zen and in its entirety was (with the opening line here being the title-misconception):

> Zen is dedicated to the experience of "sudden enlightenment," which frees its followers from the extended regimens of training in ethics, meditation, and wisdom found in conventional forms of Buddhism. Zen monks routinely expect to spend decades in full-time practice before they will be able to make real progress in their meditation.

This is a rebut to the fantasies common in Western Zen - and elsewhere in Western Buddhism (and also amongst derivative forms) - about the ease of meditational progress.

And finally, the tenth misconception given was titled, "[a]ll spiritual traditions, Buddhism included, are different paths to the same mountaintop." Here the correction offered was:

> Many great Buddhist figures, from the Japanese Zen master Dogen to the current Dalai Lama, state unequivocally that enlightenment is accessible only to those on the Buddhist path. One can only get so far (generally, rebirth in heaven) by following other religions; only Buddhism has the path to liberation from suffering. All roads may lead to the base camp, but only Buddhism leads to the summit.

The impetus for Buswell and Lopez's efforts here, and presumably in part for a number of their other works, must have been to try to correct the incredible proliferation of nonsense (usually pretentious nonsense) passing for Buddhism in the West. Perhaps out of frustration they went overboard a bit, the last point on the singular opportunity presented by Buddhist practice is questionable even from a Buddhist perspective. In general, though, the idealizations common in Western Buddhism often appear to minimize effort, ethics, and modest expectations. They also often completely pretend around the underlying transcendental religious framework, a framework centered on making the most of one's human life within a context of interconnected sequential lives. That underlying framework(s) might be grossly inaccurate and/or the corresponding Buddhists practices very problematic, but nonetheless, that is what Buddhism is about. The transcendental framework was presumably inherited in part from common premodern beliefs.

A critical look directly at the contemporary Western Buddhist scene was also provided in another *Tricycle* magazine article. That article was by a serious meditation student Eliot Fintushel and from a secular-only perspective it critiqued the selfishness and superficiality of Western teachers [Fintushel]. What was particularly significant about this very critical article was that it was written arguably about the high ground of Western Buddhism. The type of teachers critiqued had had significant meditational training and enlightenment experiences (like Fintushel). Though probably well short of traditional Asian standards, these teachers represented quite successful lay outcomes for sustained Buddhist meditational practice in the West. Yet as Fintushel pointed out such teachers:

> had fondled students, favored lovers, played fast and easy with members' land and money, were unconfessed and unrecovered alcoholics - and those were just the actionable misdeeds. In each case the devastation was proportional to the teacher's "charisma".

Yet the most telling sign of the superficial state of Western Buddhism came in an ad along the way (in the magazine version) showing a photo of a prominent American Zen teacher with the text, "Change your life in an afternoon! Unlock the Zen power in you!". With a ceiling on a teacher's vision being simply self-help, perhaps these kinds of selfish behaviors are more likely.

◆ ◆ ◆

I think that the contemporary confused state of Buddhism reflects in part the influence of science in Western culture, and along those lines Buddhism here has tended to become re-imagined as a science-kosher alternative to traditional religions. A book chronicling some of the surprisingly long history of scientific makeover efforts for Buddhism is Donald Lopez, Jr.'s, *The Scientific Buddha: His Short and Happy Life*. Such contemporary efforts are indirectly reflected in the way that Western Buddhism has become a bit of refugee camp for those fleeing Western religions, and also directly in the explicit references to science within contemporary Buddhist literature. For a number of years the following Einstein quote was prominently used by Western Buddhists and also in advertisements for the magazine *Tricycle*:

> The religion of the future will be a cosmic religion. It should transcend a personal God and avoid dogmas and theology. Covering both the natural and the spiritual, it should be based on a religious sense arising from the experience of all things, natural and spiritual as a meaningful unity. If there is any religion that would cope with scientific needs, it would be Buddhism.

Personally, I have witnessed Western Buddhists get reverential over references to Albert Einstein and have also been at Buddhist talks where prominent mention of Einstein was made. The problem as the scholar Donald Lopez made official in an article "The Scientific Buddha" is that there is no record of Einstein saying this [Lopez]. This was also apparent to the curious who simply visited the library and scoured Einstein biographies. This same non-quote is currently at the website of the physicist and author, Trinh Xuan Thuan [Thuan]. Ultimately, though, why should people care what Albert Einstein said about something that he very likely knew next to nothing about and certainly didn't practice?

Over the years, efforts to find some scientific footing for Buddhism in the West have also involved a lot of speculation based on quantum physics [Wallace 2010; Ricard and Thuan]. Somehow speculation about some of the mysteries found in the minute details of matter have great import for understanding our psyches, their mysteries, and the associated challenges. By extension, has anyone ever observed that quantum physicists seem to have a leg up with regards to the challenges of life and well-being? This same question, of course, might be asked broadly of scientists and intellectuals.

Neuroscience has recently superseded quantum speculation in the race to scientifically bolster Buddhism in the West. Preceding the contemporary wave of neuroscientists pushing mindfulness meditation, was a big effort by a longtime Zen practitioner and neurologist, James Austin. Austin has apparently been trying for decades to make brain-only sense out of some of the experiences that can arise as a result of sustained Zen meditation. In his 1998, *Zen and the Brain: Toward an Understanding of Meditation and Consciousness*, Austin worked particularly towards building a brain explanation for enlightenment experiences [Austin]. He was significantly motivated by his own brief initial enlightenment (or kensho) experience, an experience that lasted approximately 5 seconds and that he characterized with such extraordinary phrases as "Absolute Reality", "Intrinsic Rightness", and "Ultimate Perfection".

Austin's *Zen and the Brain* effort (as well as subsequent ones) are significant in part because of the relatively serious sustained efforts by the author in Zen practice and also because of their science-framed interpretations. Austin has been practicing Zen meditation since 1974 and his book's dedication included the names of three of his Japanese Zen teachers. Despite his traditional

Zen training background he completely discarded the religious content of Zen and was left with the very difficult task of making brain-only sense out of an experience of "Absolute Reality". He opened the book by positing his "straightforward thesis" that "[deep] awakening, enlightenment occurs only because the human brain undergoes substantial changes", changes which were posited to "both profoundly enhance yet simplify, the workings of the brain" [p.xix]. Does such a radical change in the brain seem feasible in a brief passive experience? Other than physical setbacks and perhaps profound psychological trauma, what significant short term changes appear possible with the brain?

Alternatively, a dualistic perspective on enlightenment (or other profound religious or mystical experiences) requires no neural changes but could follow from the soul letting go of identification with the brain's activities. Such a release could then be characterized as liberation of the immortal soul from identification with material phenomena and all the worries that go with them. Perhaps along these lines the coauthor of the *Tibetan Book of the Dead*, Tibetan Buddhist teacher Chogyam Trungpa mentioned in his commentary that "[w]hen energy becomes independent, complete energy, it begins to look at itself, which transcends the ordinary idea of perception" [p.29]. Such a breakthrough or recognition by the soul of its own intrinsic existence, as distinct from identification with neural activity (and more generally the body), could be somewhat analogous to the soul's focused functional breakthroughs previously hypothesized for episodes of acquired savant syndrome.

Another problem with Austin's modern take on Zen Buddhism is the rarity of significant enlightenment experiences. How many individuals have had the kind of profound and lasting transformation that Westerners like James Austin appear fixated on? In Philip Kapleau's classic, *Three Pillars of Zen*, there is an account of the deep enlightenment experiences of a young Japanese lay woman Yaeko Iwasaki in 1935 [Kapleau, pp. 281-304]. After 5 years of practicing Zen meditation as part of her lay life she had a rapid sequence of astonishing experiences leaving her completely overwhelmed with "tears of gratitude" and a thorough reorientation to life including an apparent appreciation of the transcendental aspect. She then died peacefully after a premonition of her pending death. The backdrop to these experiences were her correspondences with the experienced Zen teacher Harada-Roshi. Harada-Roshi acknowledged the extreme rarity of this happening as well as the relative superficiality of the more common introductory (legitimate kensho) experiences. From Austin's scientific or objective perspective then it would seem that the much sought after deep transformative awakening is a very rare occurrence and even then the affected individual will of course die. Furthermore, the associated traditional Zen training approach is apparently dying out in Japan as described in a New Yorker article [MacFarquhar].

There is a final point of significance associated with Austin's neuro-Zen work. It is an indirect one and can be found in Sam Harris' *Waking Up* [Harris S. 2014]. Harris' book was another effort to bring prominence to the scientific perspective and more particularly to extend the science-umbrella to cover select mystical or meditational phenomena (and of course to take shots at the religious). In particular Harris claimed that:

> [u]ntil we can talk about spirituality in rational terms - acknowledging the validity of self-transcendence - our world will remain shattered by dogmatism. This book has been my attempt to begin such a conversation [p.203].

What is quite impressive, even by Harris' very loose philosophical standards, is that *Waking Up* never mentions Austin despite the fact that Harris must have been aware of his work. Austin was more experienced and qualified at both ends of the proposed conversation. In fact starting in 1998 Austin published 2,140 pages on the subject (through MIT Press no less) before Harris' *Waking Up*. Furthermore amidst the decades of predominantly secular presentations of Buddhism in the West that Harris somehow neglected, there have been explicit examples of teachers overtly rejecting the religious aspects of Buddhist practice as with the late Toni Packer (starting in 1981). As a further followup comment here, dogmatism is much more prevalent and problematic than Harris implies. You can see it operating in many areas, including of course politics.

◆ ◆ ◆

The Dalai Lama has also been quite influential to framing the western Buddhist scene. In addition to his apparent inadvertent rise to celebrity-hood, he has also tried to push connections between Buddhism and science (in part through the Mind and Life Institute). The latest and most prominent contribution was probably with regards mindfulness meditation. A November 2014 *Scientific American* article, "mind of the meditator" by Matthieu Ricard, Antoine Lutz, and Richard J. Davidson described some scientific efforts to characterize the brain changes that appeared to be correlated with meditation (in particular focused-attention, mindfulness, and compassion and loving kindness). That article had opened with an acknowledgement of the Dalai Lama's foundational contributions to such investigations. The meditation article made a number of confident points on its way to some conclusions including:

> [a]bout 15 years of research have done more than show that meditation produces significant changes in both the function and structure of the brains of experienced [10,000 hours or more] practitioners. These studies are now starting to demonstrate that contemplative practices may have a substantive impact on biological processes critical for physical health.

and in closing that:

> [t]he ability to cultivate compassion and other positive human qualities lays the foundation for an ethical framework unattached to any philosophy or religion,

which could have a profoundly beneficial effect on all aspects of human societies.

The support for such assertions was overstated, though. The article seemed only loosely quantitative and the one graph purporting to show enhancement in neural features from meditation showed small effects and significant overlap between the measurements of experienced meditators and those of controls. The authors also failed to respond to a followup published letter (by a meditator) on the potential for distortion due to selection bias. The possible limitations of such studies - and contemporary neuroscience - will be discussed in the next chapter.

More seriously, though, I wondered why the meditation article didn't point out that similar and for the most part secularly-packaged meditation has been quite widely available in the West for more than 40 years? If such mediation were as productive of a lay self-help vehicle as claimed by Richard *et al* then it arguably should have sold itself - like an effective dieting routine - and had little need for neuro-scientific repackaging.

Finally evidence of the limitations of these science-connecting efforts can be found at the "North American Seat" of the Dalai Lama, Namgyal Monastery, which is located not far from me in Ithaca, New York. As I have observed, they offer Tibetan Buddhist programs which are open to the public and taught by very qualified Tibetan monks. Those programs are affordable and also presented in a very friendly atmosphere. Ithaca being home to both Ithaca College, Cornell University, and a substantial alternative community as well, would seem to be a very good location for such programs. Cornell in fact happens to be one of the top universities in terms of their funding levels from the National Science Foundation. One might then think that Namgyal's programs would draw plenty of interest. But in fact for their monthly weekend teaching programs (which open with a free Friday evening session) they send off e-advertisements until the opening day in order to try to fill their venue. That venue for years has been a modest-sized living room (in a modest-sized house). That in a nut shell I would argue reflects the status of Buddhism, as well as religious cultures including Tibetan, in the modern science-influenced, secular world. Has building bridges to science - which is fixated on scientific materialism - really helped?

But perhaps the modern secular meditation scene is doing better. In fact 60 miles west of Namgyal Monastery happens to be the Springwater Center which continues to carryout Toni Packer's completely areligious vision of meditation. Despite their cutting secular-edge history (at one point in the eighties Toni even labored through some of the early neural literature) it appears to enjoy a similar bottomline lack of participation as Namgyal's. One might then wonder if the contemporary mindfulness movement will simply pan out as just another trendy episode and not the purported "profoundly beneficial" general social development.

◆ ◆ ◆

My own observations of people who follow the religion of Buddhism have been based on some neighbors I had from Laos and also some more limited observations of Tibetans. My refugee neighbors from Laos appeared to have a strong transcendental belief in the nature of life, perhaps in part inherited from pre-Buddhist beliefs in Laos and also supported by their local spiritual traditions [Strong, pp.238-241]. One neighbor woman described her understanding of the ultimate cause of the death of some of her children and it involved the karma resulting from the actions of another family member. I found out that taking their kids to a nearby cemetery was unacceptable because of possible problems with ghosts. Their faith in Buddhism appeared to be strong, although it was ok for some of their kids to attend a Christian church with one of their sponsors. I understand that later the local Laos community built a large Buddhist temple.

The striking thing about my Laotian neighbors was that despite their challenges they managed to keep their spirits up and in fact were great neighbors to my son and me. I suspect that a significant part of their relative wellbeing arose from their Buddhist's beliefs.

This may be similar to the wellbeing boost purported for other sincere religious people. I do wonder, though, how my former neighbors, whom I have not seen in years, are faring with their religious-perspective (as well as language and cultural) challenges. Amongst the lay Tibetan people I have interacted with I have also sensed a well being and friendliness boost again perhaps connected with their Buddhist beliefs. With both the Laotian and Tibetans I have observed, I have been struck and impressed with simply their friendly and sincere presence. I have not noticed the intellectual edge or attitude that seems to underly quite a bit of the Western Buddhist movement. Additionally, with all due respect to the previously given endorsements of the high caliber of Buddhist philosophy, I think Buddhism - and certainly meditation - are minimally intellectual in nature.

WINDING DOWN

This chapter has criticized the narrowness and arrogance of modern academic science, in particular with regards to its central tenet of materialism. It also criticized the lack of effort on the part of the followers of religions to try to make some objective sense of their beliefs, and perhaps in so doing update them. If there really is something deeper going on with life it would be good to try to objectively characterize it. I also in some detail criticized the superficial state of Buddhism in the West. On a related note, for those looking for a current situation exemplifying the cultural collision between a traditional religious group and a modern secular, science-influenced group, I would suggest considering the conflict in Tibet. Both groups were on somewhat similar economic footings when China invaded Tibet and the subsequent conflict reflects some of the very different priorities found with a strongly secular versus a strongly religious mindset. It is not hard to find problems on both sides. One significant objective difference between the two groups, though, was population density. China was (and is) challenged by its very high population density, Tibet wasn't (and is not yet) challenged in this regard.

In concluding here I consider two somewhat overlapping items from the periphery of religion and science and then a key divisive issue, evolution. The first of the two concluding fringe stories here involves the late physicist David Bohm. Although a successful physicist he was largely an outsider or outcast with regards to mainstream physics, and he also had ties to modern religious figures including the neo-religious philosopher Jiddu Krishnamurti and also the Dalai Lama. In the early 1950's Bohm presented what he thought could be a coherent deterministic explanation of quantum phenomena. A possible start to a non-magical interpretation of quantum mechanics, if you will. In simple terms, Bohm followed up and extended the work published in 1927 by the physicist Louis de Broglie to suggest that underlying the apparent randomness and all-around weirdness of quantum phenomena, was a subtle force or potential that imposed wave-like movement on particles. This quantum potential was proposed to be dependent on all of the particles present and their positions.

The prominent physicist John Bell commented in 1987:

> In 1952 I saw the impossible done. It was in papers by David Bohm. Bohm showed explicitly how parameters could indeed be introduced, into nonrelativistic wave mechanics, with the help of which the indeterministic description could be transformed into a deterministic [or non-random] one. More importantly, in my opinion, the subjectivity of the orthodox version, the necessary reference to the "observer," could be eliminated. ... Why is the [de-Broglie-Bohm] pilot wave picture ignored in text books? Should it not be taught, not as the only way, but as an antidote to the prevailing complacency? To show us that vagueness, subjectivity, and indeterminism, are not forced on us by experimental facts but by theoretical choice? [Bell, p.160]

Bohm's work appeared to offer an alternative to what has ultimately produced an avalanche of hyped speculation.

In the Bohm biography, *Infinite Potential*, a friend and physicist F. David Peat chronicled the impact on Bohm of his ostracism from the academic physics community [Peat]. Bohm had initially had two disjointed expectations with regards to what he viewed as a "major discovery". One was that this would be greeted "with enthusiasm" by the physics community. The other expectation was that "the big-shots will treat my article with a conspiracy of silence; perhaps implying privately to the smaller shots that while there is nothing demonstrably illogical about the article, it is really just a philosophical point, of no practical interest" [Peat, p.125].

As the mathematician Sheldon Goldstein pointed out in reviewing Peat's book, Bohm's second expectation "[t]o a very great extent ... is what happened". As an example, his mentor the physicist Robert Oppenheimer, commented on the work "if we cannot disprove Bohm, then we must agree to ignore him" [Goldstein]. There were also some inexplicable and arrogant opinions offered. An associate of the physicist Neils Bohr, Leon Rosenfeld, found Bohm's work to be "very ingenious, but basically wrong." And the physicist Wolfgang Pauli commented that his work was "foolish simplicity," which "is of course beyond all help." Not surprisingly, there was a big impact on Bohm who at one point wrote that the physics community's indifference to this significant proposal "cut at one's insides like a hot knife being twisted inside your heart" [Peat, p.130].

Bohm was remembered by those around him "as brilliant and daring but also as extraordinarily honest, gentle and generous" [Albert]. His range of interests and intensity were exceptional. Of interest here is that his work in trying to make sense of quantum mechanics was potentially significant to both of the somewhat overlapping camps of religion and science. Yet he was arguably rejected by physicists in part for deflating the magical interpretations surrounding quantum mechanics and over the years has been ironically embraced by some Buddhists who somehow perceived his work as bolstering the intellectual credibility of Buddhism. In fact his work challenged the speculative, fantastical detours associated with quantum mechanics and as such might have prompted some Buddhists, and of course others (see for example *The God Theory* [Haisch]), to actually try to make some real-life sense out of dualistic beliefs. A personal lesson offered by Bohm's life was that attempts at transcendence via an intellectual or scientific route are extremely difficult [Peat, whole book].

There is a more subtle point with regards to Bohm's (and de-Broglie's) interpretation of quantum mechanics that is of relevance here. The posited subtle quantum force which would impart a wave-like motion on particles would conceptually be analogous to that required by a transcendental influence. If as suggested earlier there were transcendental effects - transcendental mechanics if you will - that would imply that some aspect of a soul could operate physically. Thus in a simple example the joint influence of two very close souls should somehow be able to influence a conceptus to split into two almost replicas, so as to realize their incarnation as monozygotic twins. The subsequent divergence of those twins, in particular in the health realm, would seem to require some additional subtle forces as well. Such hypothesized subtle forces could be analogous to those hypothesized in the quantum realm by De-Broglie and Bohm. A scientific explanation, on the other hand, would have to find a material-only basis for such events.

◆ ◆ ◆

The second concluding fringe example can be found in the fine 2008 book by novelist Julian Barnes, *Nothing to be frightened of* [Barnes]. Barnes' book deals with his take on death and with it quite a bit of life. The book opens with the sentence, "I don't believe in God, but I miss Him" [p.3]. The essential backdrop to the work is that Barnes has opted for an intelligent understanding of death and life which of course means science, and this is not surprisingly rather bleak. With this perspective Barnes can still intellectualize and philosophize around a bit - including taking some shots at atheists, philosophers, and more generally modern trends (although there he shortchanged frenetic distraction-ism in favor of "frenetic [commercial] materialism"), but to little end as he surmised. Here is a relevant quote:

> We discover, to our surprise, that as (Richard]) Dawkins (i.e., "Mister Meaninglessness") memorably puts it, we are "survival machines - robot vehicles blindly programmed to preserve the selfish molecules known as genes". The paradox is that individualism - the triumph of free-thinking artists and scientists - has led us to a state of self-awareness in which we can now view ourselves as units of genetic obedience. My adolescent notion of self-construction - that vaguely, Englishly, existentialist ego-hope of autonomy - could not have been further from the truth. I thought the burdensome process of growing up ended with a man standing by himself at last - *homo erectus* at full height, *sapiens* in full wisdom - a fellow now cracking the whip on his own full account. This image ... must be replaced by the sense that, far from having a whip to crack, I am the very tip of the whip itself, and that what is cracking me is a long and inevitable plait of genetic material which cannot be shrugged or fought off. My 'individuality' may still be felt, and genetically provable; but it may be the very opposite of the achievement I once took it for [p.93-94].

Further, "[n]ow, alone, we must consider what our Godless wonder might be for" [p.93]; Christianity is a "beautiful lie" [p.53]; and modern alternative pursuits - the "secular modern heaven of self-fulfillment" - and their purported realization of happiness is "our chosen myth" [p.59]. And of course, "[t]he air has been let out of the tyres of free will" [p.181].

A basic contemporary intellectual sentiment was nicely offered by a friend of Barnes' [p.124]:

> I think the theory of evolution explains it all. It's a very beautiful theory, come to think of it, a marvelous and

inspiring theory, though it has grim consequences for us.

Additionally, in a more immediate subjective sense Barnes wrote [p.148]:

> But the brain mappers who have penetrated our cerebral secrets, who lay it all out in vivid colors, who can follow the pulsings of thought and emotion, tell us that there is no one home. There is no ghost in the machine. The brain, as one neuropsychologist puts it, is no more or less than "a lump of meat".

Barnes appears to be a very perceptive person (and an excellent writer) and he nicely characterized quite a bit of the gist of the modern scientific perspective. How many educated people would question his points? In fact in a *New York Times* review Garrison Keillor commented cavalierly, "[a]ll true so far as it goes, but so what" [Keillor]. Perhaps excepting his deflation of the "modern secular heaven", isn't Barnes' take on life the only one supported in modern secular educational systems?

One interesting phenomenon presented in *Nothing to be frightened of* was Barnes' lifelong, and apparently innate, fear of death (thanatophobia). This fear also showed up in the lives of a number of his friends and was also experienced by several literary figures mentioned as well. For Barnes in addition to being a daily (and book motivating) distraction this fear also showed up in terrifying nightmares involving futile efforts to stave off death. Some of these woke Barnes up and left him and beating his "pillow with fist and shouting 'oh no Oh No OH NO' in an endless wail" [pp.124-125]. These dreams at one point were described by Barnes as involving "being chased, surrounded, outnumbered, outgunned, of finding myself bulletless, held hostage, wrongly condemned to the firing squad" [p.146]. The presumed explanation for this condition ultimately fell to DNA - "[t]hanks for the gene, Dad" [p.63].

Is it really feasible, though, that some of the DNA - or any conceivable bio-code - could specify for such tendencies, in particular for the nightmares? One transcendental explanation is that such dreams can be viewed as experienced-based, either from earlier deaths or from post-death visions. On the latter point, Barnes' nightmares appeared similar to descriptions in the *Tibetan Book of the Dead* of potential terrifying experiences faced in the transition between lives. Some of those experiences involve relentless pursuers such that one might feel "that you are being chased by various terrifying wild animals and pursued by a great army in snow, rain, storms and darkness" [Fremantle and Trungpa, p.177]. Such terrifying experiences, though, were described as a soul's "own confused projection[s]" and ultimately recognizable as such.

◆ ◆ ◆

The final point here is that the topic of evolution defines a major barrier ultimately separating the followers of religion from the followers of science. Evolution as it is taught is not an open theory about the origins of different species and their characteristics, whereby the religious might think that it does not conflict with some of their core religious beliefs. Unlike scientists studying the Earth's climate who have taken heat for their expressions concerning the uncertainty associated with warming predictions - what else could they really do? No, evolution is taught as exhibit A of the materialist vision which completely and unequivocally denies that any aspect of life is anything more than an expression of molecular interaction. Interested readers might try to find a biology textbook or even a popular book by a biologist that in any way questions this. Thus science and its followers will continue to attack religious detractors of the theory of evolution, whilst in no way acknowledging any challenges to the encompassing materialist vision. On a more subtle and heretical point, perhaps our innate understanding of an inherent design aspect of life as presented in *Born Believers* reflects subtle forces that somehow influenced mutations that in turn influenced the very complex evolutionary history. In that case, even the gross physical accuracy of the theory of evolution would only be superficial.

A closing statement on science's understanding of life comes from Ursula Goodenough's *The Sacred Depths of Nature* and it reads:

> [A]ll of us, and scientists are no exception, are vulnerable to the existential shudder that leaves us wishing that the foundations of life were something other than just so much biochemistry and biophysics. The shudder, for me at least, is different from the encounters with nihilism that have beset my contemplation of the universe. There I can steep myself in cosmic Mystery. But the workings of life are not mysterious at all. They are obvious, explainable, and thermodynamically inevitable. And relentlessly mechanical. And bluntly deterministic. My body is some 10 trillion cells. Period. My thoughts are a lot of electricity flowing along a lot of membrane. My emotions are the result of neurotransmitters squirting on my brain cells. I look in the mirror and see the mortality and I find myself fearful, yearning for less knowledge, yearning to believe that I have a soul that will go to heaven and soar with the angels [pp.46-47].

That is the scientific vision of life.

Chapter 7

Science's Problem, an Old Explanation, and Some Possible Personal Upshot

This chapter reassesses and furthers the basic points and possibilities discussed in the book and also closes with some personal observations.

Case Against Materialism

Considered herein have been some of the general implications of the unfolding DNA deficit as well as some remarkable behavioral conundrums. With this perspective, I am continually amazed at the ongoing confident presentations of, and of course allegiance to, science's number one dogma - life is completely describable as molecular/mechanical interactions. This shows up in even seemingly sympathetic articles such as in a 2014 *Atlantic* magazine article "The War on Reason" by psychologist and author Paul Bloom in which he informs readers that "[w]e are soft machines - amazing machines, but machines nonetheless" [Bloom]. Bloom's friendly materialist article was then attacked by the biologist Jerry Coyne for appearing to claim "we're not biochemical puppets because we can reason" [Coyne]. Contradicting these robotic presumptions and their associated evolutionary roots, though, are some obvious behavioral phenomena. These phenomena appear to have been selectively ignored by scientists.

A relevant example of this was found in a 2014 *Scientific American* blog entry entitled "The Mind of a Prodigy" by the psychologist Scott Barry Kaufman [Kaufman]. He wrote that "[p]eople differ in their genetic foundation, but all talents must be developed through an intricate and dynamic interplay of ability, motivation, practice, and support". He provided the following explanation of prodigies:

> [based] on detailed interviews with the children and their family members, David Henry Feldman and Lynn Goldsmith concluded that the prodigy phenomenon is the result of a lucky "coincidence" of factors, including the following: the existence of a domain matched exceptionally well to the prodigy's proclivities and interests, availability of the domain in the prodigy's geographical location, healthy social/emotional development, family aspects (birth order and gender), education and preparation (informal and formal), cultural support, recognition for achievement in the domain, access to training resources, material support from family members, at least one parent completely committed to the prodigy's development, family traditions that favor the prodigy's development, and historical forces, events, and trends.

This smorgasbord-ish assessment dodges the leviathan in the baby pool. The entire phenomenon is dependent on the mysterious existence of young super-motivated, -focused, and -capable children who appear to grossly violate science's understanding of human development.

Going further, though, Kaufman did add a genetic logic to his essay:

genes can be thought of as learning devices that predispose us to acquire certain information in the environment, and ignore other aspects of our world. Viewed in this way, genes are fundamentally active seekers of knowledge as they attempt to find the best fit to their genome. Therefore, genes exert their influences on the development of talent through the control of motivations, preferences, and emotional responses. Over time, people will accumulate experiences that result in the practice of skills, habits, and patterns of responding that reinforces the drives in an ongoing mutually reinforcing cycle. These drives apply to all areas of individual differences, including motivations, interests, personality, attitude, values, and quirky traits unique to each individual.

In contradiction to the previous excerpt here we have a pretty much all-around, behavioral genetics explanation. The point here of longterm DNA steering is not uncommon and was cited by Pinker in the context of intelligence where he claimed that the, "heritability of intelligence, for example, increases over a lifespan, and can be as high as .8 late in life" [Pinker 2002, p.375]. But does anyone really believe that deoxyribonucleic acid (DNA) could produce such far-reaching programmatic control, be so difficult to identify, and have such big monozygotic twin-contradictions? And is this steerage argument even appropriate in the case of prodigies who can seem to arrive already committed and focused?

A relevant 2014 update from the search for intelligence genes was discussed in a *Scientific American* blog entry by John Horgan [Horgan]. Horgan considered a *Proceedings of the National Academy of Sciences* report entitled, "Common genetic variants associated with cognitive performance identified using proxy-phenotype method" which had been authored by 59 researchers. Although the report sounded upbeat, Horgan focused on the questionable extent of the findings (and he also appeared to misinterpret the significance as simply being an expression of the poor methodology of behavioral geneticists). Horgan quoted *Nature*'s Ewen Callaway on the study's "maddeningly small findings":

> [t]he three variants the researchers identified were each responsible for an average of 0.3 points on an IQ test. (About two-thirds of the population score between 85 and 115.) That means that a person with two copies of each variant would score 1.8 points higher on an intelligence test than a person with none of them. To put those figures in perspective, these variants have about one-twentieth the influence on intelligence as do gene variants linked to other complex traits such as height, says Daniel Benjamin, a social scientist at Cornell University in Ithaca, New York, who co-led the study [Callaway].

From recent height genes studies this "one-twentieth" figure appears to translate to about 1 percent of the expected genetic influence. Callaway also cited the critical opinion of neurogeneticist Kevin Mitchell that, "[w]ith effects this small, the chances that they represent false positives are vastly increased".

The apparent unfolding success in the search for height genes is arguably a good counterpoint to the search for intelligence genes. Height appears to be largely inherited and consistent with this the heights of monozygotic twins are often very close. From the Minnesota Twins Study the correlation between the heights of separated-at-birth monozygotic twins was found to be 0.86 [Bouchard *et al*]. Height, or more generally length, varies within many species and thus one might expect that there are many different DNA contributions to it within the human genome. In fact the findings from the latest height-genes searches involved examining about 2 million common genetic variants amongst "the genomes of 253,288 people of European ancestry" and ultimately "identified 697 gene variants in 424 gene regions as related to height" [Dunham]. Investigators feel many of these variants could be involved in regulating skeletal growth and together the 697 variants could account for about 20 percent of the expected heritable component.

Intelligence, on the other hand, is largely a human specialty and thus as Steven Pinker pointed out, our "brain[s] [are], by any standard, an extraordinary adaptation" [Pinker 1997, p.40]. Pinker had also used the elephants' trunk as an analogous biological adaptation [Pinker 1997, p.152]. Variations in our trunks, if you will, would seem likely to be focused in the particular regions of our DNA that defined our evolutionary exit from chimpanzees. As mentioned earlier these regions are known, relatively small, and should include the blueprints responsible for our big brains. That the subset of the common genetic (or DNA) variants found within those regions appears to contribute little if any to the variation in our intelligences offers a significant challenge to the scientific vision. That this 2014 *National Academy of Sciences* report billed itself as a "substantive contribution" and claimed to demonstrate a "proxy-phenotype approach to discovering common genetic variants that is likely to be useful for many phenotypes of interest to social science (such as personality traits)" in fact more likely provides a glimpse of the frustration arising in the wake of the missing heritability problem.

The scientific community - with academia in tow - will not look outside the materialist perspective, though, so if the basis for apparent heritability lay elsewhere they are very unlikely to contemplate it. Rather, there could well be a pending very long search of other DNA-based candidates. As previously mentioned the prominent geneticist J. Craig Venter commented on the current deficit in personal genomics saying that, "[a]nything short of [whole genome] sequencing is going to be short on accuracy - and even then, there's almost no comprehensive data sets to compare to" [Piekoff]. I suspect that the availability of such whole genome analyses along with "comprehensive data sets" is not likely to happen for a long time. Even then with relatively rare events such as the transgender phenomenon, the limited statistics could well undermine confidence in a DNA contribution. Moreover with consideration being given to an "infinitesimal model" - involving very tiny contributions summed across many, many DNA variants - even "with comprehensive data sets" definitive answers might be difficult to confirm. Further, any pending genetic searches could end up being a prelude to extended searches for epigenetic and/or subtle environmental origins. Finally, it is difficult to imagine that relevant scientists will ask hard questions about how this unfolding iffy DNA picture is going to be able to deliver answers for exceptional behavioral tendencies.

◆ ◆ ◆

On somewhat of a parallel trajectory could be neuroscience's search for the brain/neural dynamics presumed to underlie the totality of our mental experiences. To some this possible proof that our minds are nothing more than the functioning of our brains is the ultimate test of the materialist position, but this misses underlying questions about the heritability of our individual mental tendencies. Materialism demands material-only descriptions of both the inheritance process and the supporting neural-molecular dynamics.

Neuroscience's complete confidence in the materialist vision is not hard to find, even in a friendly clinically-oriented book like V. S. Ramachandran's (with S. Blakeslee) *Phantoms in the Brain* [Ramachandran]. In that book readers are informed that over the "last three decades" (circa 1998) neuroscientists "have learned a great deal about the laws of mental life and about how these laws emerge from the brain" [p.256]. Ramachandran wrote about the "exhilarating" progress that had been made but acknowledged that this process had left many "uncomfortable". As he wrote:

> [i]t seems somehow disconcerting to be told that your life, all your hopes, triumphs and aspirations simply arise from the activity of neurons in your brain. But far from being humiliating, this idea is ennobling, I think. Science - cosmology, evolution and especially the brain sciences - is telling us that we have no privileged position in the universe and that our sense of having a

private nonmaterial soul "watching the world" is really an illusion [p.256].

Ramachandran went on to offer an additional consolation that this apparent selfless nihilism was consistent with an intellectual take on "Eastern mystical traditions". Somehow we should feel "liberat[ed]" and "ennobl[ed]" that we can partake in this parade of intellectual certainty and simultaneously score some "Eastern mystical" points. From such sentiments you can sense some of the continuity and perhaps predictability of Sam Harris' subsequent *Waking Up* effort. Furthermore, it is noteworthy that once again when a scientist puts a positive spin on the materialist perspective they neglect to mention the sober import for their own perspective. That is according to materialism, what exactly is creativity?

In any case Ramachandran's certainty was inappropriate and the March 2014 issue of *Scientific American* had a fine update on the 2014-ish state of neuro-scientific inquiry by Rafael Yuste and George M. Church [Yuste and Church]. Following a big splashy title of "The New Century of the Brain - Big Science lights the way to an understanding of how the world's most complex machine gives rise to our thoughts and emotions", was a very sober layout of how little is currently known and how much in the way of technical developments appears to be needed. Those developments would be focused on recording and controlling the activity in the brain's labyrinth of circuits. The authors plunged into their formidable task by offering some sober assessments. Their opening paragraph read:

> Despite a century of sustained research, brain scientists remain ignorant of the workings of the three-pound organ that is the seat of all conscious activity. Many have tried to attack this problem by examining the nervous systems of simpler organisms. In fact, almost 30 years have passed since investigators mapped the connections among each of the 302 nerve cells in the round worm Caenorhabditis elegans. Yet the worm-wiring diagram did not yield an understanding of how these connections give rise to even rudimentary

behaviors such as feeding and sex. What was missing were data relating the activity of neurons to specific behaviors.

They went on to point how superficial and deceptive popular presentations of human brain experiments can be. Commenting on one popular story, the authors wrote:

> A noteworthy example of the mismatch is a much publicized study identifying single brain cells that fired an electrical impulse in response to the face of actor Jennifer Aniston. Despite the hoopla, the discovery of a "Jennifer Aniston neuron" was something like a message from aliens, a sign of intelligent life in the universe but without any indication about the meaning of the transmission. We are still completely ignorant of how the pulsing electrical activity of that neuron influences our ability to recognize Aniston's face and then relate it to a clip from the television show *Friends*. For the brain to recognize the star, it probably has to activate a large ensemble of neurons, all communicating using neural code that we have yet to decipher.

On a related note *Scientific American* also had a February 2013 article entitled "Brain Cells for Grandmother" by the experimenters who had encountered in one patient the apparent "Jennifer Aniston neuron" (which also responded to another costar from the TV series *Friends*), and that article discussed this discovery and its possible implications for memory [Quiroga *et al*].

Overall, Yuste and Church claimed that for neuroscience to fundamentally advance it:

> needs a new set of technologies that will enable investigators to monitor and also alter the electrical activity of thousands or even millions of neurons - techniques capable of deciphering what the Spanish neuroanatomist Santiago Ramon y Cajal called 'the

impenetrable jungles where many investigators have lost themselves'.

Penetrating those jungles, though, as outlined in the Yuste and Church article is likely to be a monumental task. Along the way if researchers can create the requisite technologies then they can scale up the brains examined. Even with a mouse's brain, though, such efforts "could generate 300 terabytes of compressed data in an hour". The pending enormous challenges led the authors to the plea-ful conclusion:

> We need collaboration among academic disciplines. Building instruments to image voltage in millions of neurons simultaneously throughout entire brain regions may be achieved only by a sustained effort of a large interdisciplinary team of researchers. The technology could then be made available at a large-scale, observatory-like facility shared by the neuroscience community. We are passionate about retaining a focus on new technology to record, control and decode the patterns of electrical spikes that are the language of the brain. We believe that without these new tools, neuroscience will remain bottlenecked and fail to detect the brain's emergent properties that underlie a virtually infinite range of behaviors. Enhancing the ability to understand and use the language of spikes and neurons is the most productive way to derive a grand theory of how nature's most complex machine functions.

Additional complexity appears to have been neglected here, though. In the end whatever is recorded with regards to an individual's brain activity will also have to be compared against that individual's limited recollection and description of their concurrent subjective mental experience. An experience which would necessarily be a static one within an "observatory-like facility".

While Yuste and Church's approach might provide meaningful insight into phenomena akin to celebrity recognition, what meaningful chunk of our "virtually infinite range of behaviors" could be observed and also have their neural correlates clearly identified amidst the ongoing sea of concurrent brain activity, perhaps much of it associated with unconscious processes (including body-directed processing)? What if the observed person was experiencing something that did not have neural correlates? How would that be distinguished amidst the inevitable concurrent neural activity? Given the fixed neuroscience position that brain activity defines the mind, it is difficult to conceive of a scenario in which neuroscientists would contemplate beyond the neural data for an explanation. Even in prominent cases of near death experiences involving patients apparently lacking vital signs, extra-neural hypotheses are simply dismissed.

It is also of note here that this enormous complexity and ambiguity does not bolster confidence in optimistic brain-based claims, like those found in the earlier considered "mind of the meditator" article.

Also missing in such neuro-analyses are some of the existing gross challenges to brain-based reasoning. For some time now it has been apparent that some individuals can function very well despite having very little brain tissue. As a result of the condition hydrocephalus, some people have had their brain's cerebrospinal fluid reservoirs (or ventricles) enlarge and thus displace and destroy other brain tissues. In a 1980 *Science* article, "Is Your Brain Really Necessary?", some significant findings on this condition by British neurologist John Lorber were discussed [Lewin]. In breaking down over 600 scans of patients with spina bifida - most of whom also had hydrocephalus - into categories based on the fraction of the cranium (or braincase) occupied by cerebrospinal fluid, of note were the scans in which in order to hold the increased fluid levels, "ventricle expansion fill[ed] 95 percent of the cranium". This category included "less than 10 percent" of the 600-plus patients. Within this category it was noted that "many" of these affected individuals were:

severely disabled, but half of them have IQ's greater than 100. This group provide[d] some of the most dramatic examples of apparent normal function against all odds.

One particularly dramatic example was described in a quote from Lorber:

> [t]here is a young student at [Sheffield University] who has an IQ of 126, has gained a first-class honors degree in mathematics, and is socially completely normal. And yet the boy has virtually no brain.

What do neuroscientists think they would find at some future "observatory-like facility" when examining an individual like this? Further, if Lorber observed that a significant fraction of very small-brained people managed to obtain normal mental functioning then why wouldn't a decent fraction of the rest of us with our regular-sized brains likewise function at extraordinary levels?

Additional observations by Lorber pertained to a subgroup of patients for whom their ventricle expansion had been limited to one side of the brain. Lorber pointed out that:

> I've now seen more than 50 cases of [such] asymmetrical hydrocephalus and the interesting thing is that only a minority of these individuals show the expected and long-cherished neurological finding of paralysis with spasticity on the opposite side of the body.

Lorber then went on to point out that one of these patients displayed spastic paralysis on the *same* side as their "enormously enlarged ventricles". Why haven't such findings found their way into the popular neuroscience coverage? Why didn't Darold Treffert discuss these findings as a counterpoint to his brain abnormalities-based explanation of savant behaviors, much of it based on the logic of hemispheric specialization? Do any recent neuroscience books even mention Lorber's findings?

I finish up critiquing science's materialist vision with a further note on its prevalence. Other than perhaps a few singular islands such as at the University of Virginia, I am not aware of any work within academia that seriously questions the materialist view. There still may be some philosophers finding intellectual reasons to question the presumed lack of free will, but without questioning the underlying material-only foundation, these reasons can be easily dismissed as superficial rationalizations. Even Thomas Nagel's suggested challenge to materialism - which drew enormous academic flak - was simply an argument for a deeper vision of materialism. In it some deeper layer of physical reality was essential to the development of consciousness. If Nagel is right then perhaps at some large "observatory-like [or particle physicists' CERN-like] facility" in the future scientists will see some objective support for his claim - perhaps in the form of a Nagel Particle. Further, even in the case of religion-based efforts like those of Stephen C. Meyer, the apparent goal is simply to find evidence of some divine intervention in the chain that led to the current robotic regime. Has anyone in the contemporary academic realm raised as general and intuitive protest against the materialist view as that given in the 1600's by Joseph Glanvill in the quote from Chapter 1 based on the readily apparent differences between monozygotic twins?

An Old Explanation

The origins of my interest in a transcendental view are personal. As a young child I had repeated intense dreams which had no apparent connection to my life. I also experienced a deep phobia. Together with some features of my body I sensed a connection to someone who had died in a difficult scenario. As an adult I noted some agreement between these observations and the cases suggestive of reincarnation considered by the late Ian Stevenson. Then later I read some details of how a group faced a challenging situation in which some likely died and this immediately struck a chord. Not only was the dying scenario consistent with my own assessment, but more generally there was prominent continuity between my life's trajectory and the interests and priorities of that group. My immediate impression was that this kind of apparent transcendental connection could be a general one and thus the common premodern beliefs.

From personal experiences I think the early childhood years represent a profound shift. The underlying soul becomes increasingly accustomed to the brain and body, and simultaneously the previous very different disembodied experience fades out. This is roughly consistent with the earlier given quote by the Indian man who had commented that young children "had not yet forgotten or grown confused and distracted by the world" [Barrett, p.2]. From some personal observations, I suggest that eventually there is a fearful transition in which the identification with the body and its apparent mortality becomes essentially complete, leaving only a slight sense of dualism which is the basis of our religious instincts. Furthermore, this transition could be coincident with the mysterious onset of childhood amnesia in which we lose personal memories of our first three or four years [Tucker 2005, p.90]. Thus childhood amnesia could be an artifact of the soul's repression of its memories of the previous disembodied experience. From this perspective I think that memories of previous (embodied) lives are very rare since our conscious experiences tend to be bracketed between the sequential and profoundly different bodied and dis-embodied realms. Once we make one of those huge transitions then little from the previous complementary existence - let alone anything that preceded it - matters. Our ship has sailed.

On a related aside, the life-changing effects attributed to near-death experiences could have a transcendental explanation. That is those effects could be seen as the fallout associated with an adult having plunged back into the very different disembodied realm. Obtaining a concurrent psyche-grip on both of these realms could be very difficult. Also the apparent personal and/or cultural conditioning found with near-death experiences could simply be an expression of the soul's conditioning, a conditioning that is also expressed in the continuity of behavior across lives. Furthermore, the life-recall sometimes experienced in near-death experiences could be seen as an expression of the extraordinary memory of the soul, a memory that also appears to be displayed in part amongst the living, including cases of hyperthymesic syndrome.

As previously suggested an incarnating soul could be drawn to their subsequent parents and this could account for the rough patterns of heredity, patterns that have led to the ongoing DNA searches. One description of some Buddhist views of this possible human incarnation process was found in a passage of B. Alan Wallace's *Meditations of a Buddhist Skeptic*:

> According to the Buddha, three things are necessary for the emergence of a human psyche and the formation of a human embryo: ovulation on the part of the mother, the parent's sexual intercourse, and the presence of a being in the intermediate state (between lives) who has the karma to be reborn to specific parents at a particular time. Such beings in the intermediate state are certainly influenced by their karma, or actions in their past lives, but their own inclinations also influence the selection of the parents to whom they will be reborn. The general principle in Buddhism is that sentient beings are driven by desire to take rebirth, and when desire is accompanied by craving, hostility, and delusion, the results are painful [Wallace 2012, p.103].

Of additional note here is that at least officially, Buddhism claims that the likelihood of a human rebirth is exceedingly small. This logic is certainly challenged in modern times, though, as our population has climbed past 7 billion.

A general transcendental draw to parents could be consistent with both the heredity effects for which the DNA has been identified and also presumed heredity effects for which has no DNA basis has been found. In the latter case a behavioral tendency - say the inclination towards aggressive behavior - might not have a DNA basis, but its expression in one or more of the parents could still provide a draw to an incarnating being who themselves was inclined towards aggression. Also the similarity in the appearances of most monozygotic twins suggests that certain outcomes like appearance might be independent of a soul's trajectory, and given at least in large part by DNA. Unless both souls had recently been monozygotic twins together, it is hard to contemplate how they would otherwise have jointly had the same trajectory towards a particular appearance. From a transcendental perspective, subtle continuity- or karma-driven effects would have to somehow be responsible for the DNA-free innate aspects of an individual.

◆ ◆ ◆

Moving on to the topic of free will. Here I will base my comments in part on the definition offered by *The Columbia Encyclopedia* which says that this entails "an individual, regardless of forces external to him[/her], can and does choose at least some of his[/her] actions" [Columbia]. This definition has to be amended, though, by adding "and (material) internal" to the forces considered. Obviously if DNA is influencing decisions then that would not be free will. Conveniently, the theoretical connection between the capacity for free will and a materialist understanding of life is simple. If a material-only understanding of life is verified then free will would be impossible. Machines do not have free will, or a self for that matter. Their dynamics are simply defined by the physical interactions of their constituent elements. Thus the confidence of materialists in denying the existence of free will. In making arguments against the materialist view this book has thus indirectly helped open a door to some possible support for the existence of free will. Of particular note, simply the neural-deficit observations of Lorber appear to offer a significant challenge to a brain-only understanding of mental functioning including free will. With large portions of their brains missing, how is it that such individuals can function normally including of course make decisions? How would brain-imaging of such an individual allow for deciphering their decision making process?

Opposing any exercise of free will is our self-evident inclination towards habitual actions. This inclination should in part be due to the conditioned material aspects of our bodies and brains, beginning with our innate disposition towards pleasure and away from pain. Such material-based draws could then be argued to support a larger framework for our decisions and behaviors. The deeper questions with regards to free will, though, appear to pertain to what people do with their lives - whether in a lifestyle or a career sense - and also perhaps with regards to crisis situations. Without some DNA and/or convincing environmental support the materialist explanation runs into problems here. Consider for example the splits apparent between monozygotic twins and more generally the large variations found in the trajectories of siblings. In a simple gross sense, a transcendental perspective offers continuity across lives with an underlying (and unspecified) free will as an explanation. A person apparently born in pursuit of a piano-playing career could then be an expression of their soul's very willful commitment to playing the piano. In a previous human incarnation that soul could have become infatuated with the piano and that connection carried over strongly. In their current life or a subsequent human one, their soul could switch commitments and then perhaps pursue economics as a passion. Also of note is that from this perspective a strongly criminally-inclined individual would not have a defense based on their DNA specifics.

There should also be significant complexity in a transcendental expression of free will. As aforementioned with regards to savants, a transcendental explanation would seem to have to involve the potential for amplification coming out of the disembodied state. The challenge here is to account for the seemingly innate super-focus of some individuals (as was posited above in the piano-playing example). As was suggested earlier, a transcendental explanation could involve something akin to catching "a resonance ... in a physics sense". Somehow then it would seem that a soul's reincarnation could go overboard by focusing or willing too much on one particular interest or desire. Such a dynamic could then be very crudely consistent with the general dying strategy conveyed in the *The Tibetan Book of the Dead*, in which it is viewed as very important to approach death with your proverbial mental stuff together. An alternative given there is to have others recite that book in the hope of it helping to at least facilitate a good rebirth decision. Further potential insight into free will from a transcendental perspective is with regards to our sense of its general availability. The inclination or sense that there always is an underlying "me" freely making decisions could be seen as in part reflecting our experiences in the disembodied state. In that state a soul might encounter many opportunities or choices in a context of little or nothing in the way of external influences. Consistent with such a scenario the following TBD excerpt contains instructions to the recently deceased person:

> O child of noble family, 'without obstruction' means that you are a mental body and your mind is separated from its support, you have no material body, so now you can pass back and forth even through Mount Meru, the king of mountains, or anywhere except your mother's womb ... This is a sign that you are wondering in the bardo of becoming [Fremantle and Trungpa, p.173].

And further instructions to the deceased included:

> O child of noble family, 'possessing the power of miracles resulting from karma' means that now you have miraculous powers resulting from the force of karma in accordance with your actions, not those which come from meditation or virtues. You can circle the four continents and Mount Meru in an instant, and arrive anywhere you want instantaneously as soon as you think of it, or in the time it takes a man to stretch out and draw back his hand. But these various powers are unsuitable; do not think about them. Now you have the ability to display them without hindrance, you can

perform everything you think of and there is no action
you cannot do .... [pp.173-174]

Here and elsewhere the TBD portrays the disembodied state as
offering enormous freedom and power (as well as encountering
unverifiable elements), but warns against utilizing that capacity
since you are still bound up in your ignorance. It is this claimed
underlying freedom in the disembodied state that could be seen
here as contributing to our very generous sense of free will.

The more pervasive question about free will is also the ongoing
one. Is it possible for an individual to get beyond the superficial and
conditioned (and possibly material-only) amidst everyday life? I
think that it is possible but difficult and further I think that in
general we can intuit this possibility and challenge. This underlying
challenge is perhaps fundamental to a meaningful life. I think that
our innate sense of the capacity to "hang in there" and make
difficult decisions and then live them through could overlap with
our deeper and non-material aspects including the capacity for free
will (and perhaps love). Some remarkable and relevant examples
can be found in the book *And There Was Light* by Jacque Lusseyran
[Lusseyran]. Lusseyran had been blinded in an accident as a youth
but went on to lead an extraordinary life which included significant
roles as a teenager in the French resistance during World War II
and then during 15 months in the Buchenwald concentration camp.
His ability to sense deeper and seemingly unconditioned aspects of
life within himself - including notably the light-business and a form
of vision - and then go on living accordingly was stunning and I
suggest went beyond the limits of any material-only understanding
of life. It is difficult to imagine that any "observatory-like facility"
could have made pre-determination observations of Lusseyran as
he plunged within himself to find joy, wisdom, and immense
compassion which served to frame and direct his activities at the
Buchenwald concentration camp.

Finally, Lusseyran in his Epilogue offered the following
attribution to the extraordinary experiences of his youth:

[h]ere my story ends, as it must, for the man I am now, husband, father, university professor, writer, has no intention of telling you about himself. He wouldn't know how, and he would only burden you. If he has recorded the first twenty years of his life at such length, it is because he believes they no longer belong to him as an individual but are an open book, for anyone to read who cares to. His dearest wish was to show, if only in part, what these years held of life, light and joy, by the grace of God [pp. 279-280].

His attribution to the "grace of God" is certainly not consistent with a philosopher's take on free will, but whatever their ultimate origins, the capacities he demonstrated amidst his altruistic efforts were exceptional (even drawing a comment of "most beautiful" from Oliver Sacks) and I think challenged materialism and its denial of free will. He and many of his resistance friends appeared to be Christians by their own understandings. Finally, perhaps his experiences simply highlighted the human capacity to find liberation from our material constraints and in so doing make meaningful decisions independently of our materialist framework.

Some Possible Personal Import

The main point of this book has been to point out some basic problems with the material-only vision of life. Readers are free to do what they want with these points including of course coming up with their own explanations for some of the mysteries considered herein. I think the premodern transcendental perspective offers some simple explanations and coherence - and of course it also raises additional mysteries. I utilized some literature describing possible individual cases of reincarnation and also some relevant Buddhist literature. There has to be much more relevant literature out there for additional investigations - transcendental-oriented and otherwise.

For the curious there are many mysteries surrounding life to wonder about and a number of these offer challenges to materialism. Here it might be worth remembering what the thoughtful physicist David Bohm suggested when he wrote that 'all descriptions are incomplete' [Bohm and Peat]. Any particular explanation or perspective - including one from an established religion - is bound to be limited. For those trying to investigate possible challenges to materialism, I doubt you will find significant shared interest amongst the followers of established religions, though. I have yet to encounter a Buddhist expressing interest in investigating the possible objective basis for a transcendental vision (although I have seen some Buddhists books citing Ian Stevenson's work). My own experiences have suggested that curiosity about such matters is minimal amongst followers of religion. Additionally, amongst scientists and academics - and their followers - materialism simply isn't questioned.

In describing a few of the conundrums science faces and also some potential transcendental explanations, the scope here has been mostly limited to humans. I think that a transcendental process would have to be general and not species-bound, with a common thread perhaps being the expression of personality. There was one example given in Jim Tucker's *Life Before Life* in which a young child expressing an apparent recall of a previous life also made a reference to a previous sibling having been reborn as a fish [Tucker 2005, p.142]. The historical growth in humanity's population would have required an influx of souls. Perhaps then once on board the human incarnation circuit, a soul could tend to stick around, although some intervening stints back in the animal realm would still be possible.

I have seen in print more than once an estimate of the total number of human births during our history. That figure was 100 billion. Thus possible contemporary effects based on continuity from previous human lives could have derived from a large historical pool. One related question would be - what is the average time between incarnations, in particular, human incarnations? It would seem that in order to get significant behavioral continuity within groups (as considered in Chapter 5), you might need to have modest-sized incarnation gaps. Would showing up as a Korean every 300 years facilitate much adhesion to a Korean identity? An additional point here is that there might be other incarnation options available to a soul. In Buddhist literature there is mention of the human realm and the animal realm, but there are also four other realms described (including a realm of gods). The possibility of such realms could greatly increase the complexity of a transcendental dynamic. To further complicate transcendental contemplation, some Buddhist literature describes some incarnations as simply involving "projection bodies". Is this supposed to imply virtual doubles? My own view is that a transcendental soul would represent something element-like and of course be a singular entity.

I think that a transcendental view offers a deeper perspective on life, both with regards to our own experiences and also in relating to the lives of others. Perhaps by building some rational support for this old perspective, it might also provide a motivational boost with regards to our growing sustainability crisis. Somewhat consistent with this in Michael Tobias's man-versus-nature epic, *World War III*, the group identified for their sustainability priorities were the lay Jains, who believe that a way to liberation is to live a harmless life [Tobias].

On a conceptual or intellectual plane a transcendental connection would open up many possibilities. These include an underlying complementary aspect of reality involving eternal souls; a rational foothold for religious beliefs and experiences - at least on the soul-side; and a big backdrop for a number of science-taboo topics including near-death experiences. Perhaps consistent with such an undetectable realm of souls are the mysterious missing aspects of the inferable universe - dark matter and dark energy. It would also suggest that people long ago came upon something fundamental, itself apparently heresy amongst modern intellectuals. Although, I think the top down or God aspect of religion is in some fundamental way accurate, I also see little objective traction currently available. Making a case for the existence of souls appears to be much easier than for the existence of God or gods.

◆ ◆ ◆

Finally, I add some transcendental-related personal observations. In part motivated by this premodern perspective, I have found that a move towards a more sustainable lifestyle has been not been difficult. One aspect of this has been the adoption of a plant-based diet which appears to offer health benefits that might be consistent with the subtle cause-and-effect logic [Campbell, McDougall]. Much more challenging has been following up on the possible deeper implications of a transcendental perspective. Years ago I remember hearing about how one man who had been involved with a Zen center (which I believe at the time at least provided lip-service to a transcendental view) had answered questions about his own involvement with such a fringe group. He had simply and directly responded 'I'm trying to learn how to avoid being an asshole'. That emphasis - perhaps also shared with many religious perspectives (albeit usually in more polite terms) - has been bolstered within me as I have waded into the support for, and implications of, a transcendental component of life. This has increased my emphasis on trying to help out and also - somewhat in tandem - trying to relate with, and learn from, the ongoing experiences of life. These efforts are much more difficult than pruning one's energy usage, but they are also more rewarding.

A transcendental perspective could also have implications for very difficult circumstances. On this point the famous intellectual question framed in Shakespeare's *Hamlet* was incorrect. From a transcendental perspective it is not possible to "not be" and thus the 'ending it all'-reasoning associated with suicide is mistaken (I do not, though, see this as supportive of the modern mania to extend people's lives at great cost). From a transcendental perspective it would seem appropriate to try to learn your lessons - perhaps in particular the difficult ones - in part simply to improve your future lives. An additional option available is to partake in some religious practices so as to possibly help yourself deal with the potentially tumultuous disembodied period (remember the aforementioned nightmares of the author Julian Barnes). I wonder if an understated rationale for simple religious practices - such as prayers or the recitations of mantras - is to help with post-death stability (as well as perhaps enhancing it during difficult embodied episodes).

Years ago I had inferred some positives associated with a transcendental perspective in the lives of some of my neighbors from Laos. Perhaps more generally this overlaps with the positive effects that can be found with other sincere religious people. An underlying religious perspective on life and its challenges might be more than a helpful exercise in delusions; it might make objective sense. It would also be at odds with our increasingly distracted norms and also the intellectual focus of science and academia.

About the Author

Ted Christopher lives in Rochester, New York. He has held a variety of jobs including some academic-based, biomedical ultrasound efforts. Post-high school, his formal education has been mostly technical and included a PhD in Electrical Engineering. Concurrent with these efforts he has tried to make sense of some basic aspects of life, perhaps influenced by his involvement with Buddhist practices and more generally his religious instincts. He maintains a simple website with some relevant commentary and examples, www.scientific-heresy.info.

Acknowledgments

The author gratefully acknowledges the Central Library of Rochester and Monroe County. A number of relevant books were obtained at that library. In some cases such books were first encountered on one of Central's new books tables. The librarian Andrew Coyle was particularly helpful in obtaining books and also provided some suggestions. Central Library also offered a good reading space.

Some editing feedback was provided by Cindi Rittenhouse and also by Peter Christopher. I am very grateful for their efforts but take complete responsibility for all remaining errors.

References

Albert D. Z. Bohm's Alternative to Quantum Mechanics. *Scientific American*, May 1994. Available at www-f1.ijs.si/~ramsak/ teaching/bohm.pdf . Accessed on March 31, 2015.

Alexander E., MD. *Proof of Heaven: A Neurosurgeon's Journey into the Afterlife*. New York, NY: Simon and Schuster Paperbacks; 2012.

Alford J. R., Funk C. L., and Hibbling J. R. Are Political Orientations Genetically Transmitted? *American Political Science Review*, May 2005.

Andreadis A. blogs.scientificamerican.com/guest-blog/2012/ 09/17/junk-dna-junky-pr/ Accessed on April 4, 2015.

Angier N. In a Helpless Baby, the Roots of Our Social Glue? *New York Times*, March 3, 2009.

Angier N. Even Among Animals: Leaders, Followers and Schmoozers. *New York Times*, April 5, 2010.

Austin J. *Zen and the Brain: Toward an Understanding of Meditation and Consciousness*. Cambridge, MA: The MIT Press; 1998. An 844 page effort, so much for the Zen tendency towards minimization.

Barnes J. *Nothing to be Frighten of*. New York, NY: Alfred A. Knopf; 2008.

Barrett J. L. *Born Believers - The Science of Children's Religious Belief*. New York, NY: Free Press; 2012.

Bell J. *Speakable and Unspeakable in Quantum Mechanics*. New York, NY: Cambridge Univ. Press; 1987.

Betzig L. L. The Son Also Rises. *Evolutionary Psychology*, 5(4), 733-739. Available at www.epjournal.net/wp-content/uploads/ep05733739.pdf. Accessed on March 14, 2015.

Blau E. *Stories of Adoption: Loss and Reunion*. Troutdale, OR: New Sage Press; 1993.

Bohm D. and Peat F. D. *Science, Order, and Creativity: A Dramatic New Look at the Creative Roots of Science and Life*. New York, NY: Bantam; 1987.

Bouchard T. J., Lykken D. T., McGue M., Segal N. L., and Tellegen A. Sources of Human Psychological Differences: The Minnesota Study of Twins Reared Apart. *Science, 250*, October 12, 1990. Online at web.missouri.edu/~segerti/100H/Bouchard.pdf Accessed on February 8, 2015.

Burpo T. *Heaven is for Real*. Nashville, TN: Thomas Nelson; 2010.

Buswell R. E., Jr., and Lopez D. S., Jr. www.tricycle.com/blog/10-misconceptions-about-buddhism. Accessed on April 6, 2015.

Callaway E. www.nature.com/news/smart-genes-prove-elusive-1.15858#/ Accessed on February 8, 2015.

Campbell T. C. and Campbell T. M. *The China Study*. Dallas, TX: Benbella Books; 2004.

Christensen K., Johnson T. E., and Vaupel J. W. The quest for genetic determinants of human longevity: challenges and insights. *Nature Review Genetics* 2006,7: 436-447.

Christopher T. Premodern Transcendental Perspectives on the Missing Heritability Problem and Some Intelligence Conundrums. The correctly formatted version is available at, www.scribd.com/doc/161425585/Premodern-Transcendental-Perspectives-on-the-Missing-Heritability-Problem-and-Some-Intelligence-Conundrums Accessed on February 8, 2015. The associated poor reader score (SIQ) at Cureus was the result of the scoring of only 3 readers (or nominal readers) as was pointed out to the author by Cureus personnel.

Clark G. *A Farewell to Alms: A Brief Economic History of the World.* Princeton, NJ: Princeton University Press; 2007.

Collins F. *The Language of Life: DNA and the Revolution in Personalized Medicine.* New York, NY: HarperCollins; 2010.

The Columbia Encyclopedia. New York, NY: Columbia University Press; 2000.

Coyne J. whyevolutionistrue.wordpress.com/2014/02/24/paul-bloom-claims-that-were-not-biochemical-puppets-because-we-can-reason-hes-wrong/ Accessed on March 31, 2015.

Dawkins R. *The Selfish Gene.* New York, NY: Oxford University Press; 1976.

Dobbs, D. If Smart is the Norm, Stupidity Gets More Interesting. *New York Times*, October 22, 2012.

Dreyfus C. Alan Alda, Spokesman for Science. *New York Times*, February 24, 2014.

Dunham W. Tall tale: scientists unravel the genetics of human height. www.reuters.com/article/2014/10/05/us-science-height-idUSKCN0HU0QI20141005. Accessed on March 14, 2015.

Edsall T. B. Are Our Political Beliefs Encoded in Our DNA? *New York Times*, October 1, 2012.

Eldridge S. *Twenty Things Adopted Kids Wish Their Adoptive Parents Knew.* United States: Bantom Dell; 1999.

Fintushel E. www.tricycle.com/feature/something-offer. Accessed on April 6 2015.

Flynn J. R. Thinking in More Sophisticated Ways. *New York Times*, February 27, 2012.

Folger, T. Can We Keep Getting Smarter? *Scientific American*, September 2012.

Fox M. *Religion, Spirituality and the Near-Death Experience*. New York, NY: Routledge; 2003.

Fremantle F. and Trungpa C. *The Tibetan Book of the Dead* (pocket version). Boston, MA: Shambhala Publications; 1992.

Frenkel E. Is the Universe a Simulation? *New York Times*, February 14, 2014.

Gibson G. Rare and common variants: twenty arguments. *Nature Review Genetics* 2012, 13:135-145.

Goldstein S. A Theorist Ignored. *Science*, v. 275, 28 March 1997, p. 1893. Available at www.mathematik.uni-muenchen.de/ ~bohmmech/BohmHome/files/A_Theorist_Ignored.pdf. Accessed on March 31, 2015.

Goodenough U. *The Sacred Depths of Nature*. New York, NY: Oxford University Press; 1998.

Gottfredson L. S. The General Intelligence Factor. *Scientific American Presents - Intelligence*, Winter Quarter 1999.

Gottfredson L. S. The World Grows More Complex. *New York Times*, February 27, 2012.

Green E. D. Human Genome, Then and Now. *New York Times*, April 15, 2013.

Haisch B. *The God Theory*. San Francisco, CA: Weiser Books; 2006.

Hall S. S. Revolution Postponed. *Scientific American*, October 2010.

Harris J. R. *No Two Alike*. New York, NY: W. W. Norton & Company; 2006.

Harris S. *Free Will*. New York, NY: Free Press; 2012.

Harris S. *Waking Up*. New York, NY: Simon & Schuster; 2014.

Head J. and Cranston S. L. *Reincarnation in World Thought*. New York, NY: Julian Press; 1967.

Highfield R. and Carter P. *The Private Lives of Albert Einstein*. New York, NY: St. Martins Press; 1994.

Holden J. M., EdD, Greyson B., MD, and James D., MSN, RN. *The Handbook of Near-Death Experiences*. Santa Barbara, CA: Praeger Publishers; 2009.

Holland J. S. *Unlikely Friendships*. New York, NY: Workman Publishing; 2011.

Horgan J. blogs.scientificamerican.com/cross-check/2014/10/14/quest-for-intelligence-genes-churns-out-more-dubious-results/ Accessed on February 8, 2015.

Isaacson W. *Einstein: His Life and Universe*. New York, NY: Simon & Schuster; 2007.

Jackson M. Meow Mix. *Wildlife Conservation*, April 2001.

Jacobs G. H. and Nathans J. The Evolution of Primate Color Vision. *Scientific American*, April 2009.

Jones M. Why a Generation of Adoptees is Returning to South Korea. *New York Times Magazine*, January 18, 2015.

Juno. The deliver-and-you-are-done paradigm conveyed in the movie "Juno" is not realistic.

Kapleau P. *Three Pillars of Zen*. Garden City, NY: Anchor Books; 1980.

Kaufman S. B. The Mind of the Prodigy. blogs.scientificamerican.com/beautiful-minds/2014/02/10/the-mind-of-the-prodigy/ Accessed on March 14, 2015.

Keillor G. Dying of the Light. *New York Times Book Review*, October 5, 2008.

Kelly E. F., Kelly E. W., Crabtree A., Gauld A., Grosso M., and Greyson B. *Irreducible Mind: Toward a Psychology for the 21st Century.* Lanham, MD: Rowman & Littlefield Publishers; 2007.

Kingsley D. M. From Atoms to Traits. *Scientific American,* January 2009.

Kinn G. *Be My Baby: Parents and Children Talk About Adoption.* New York, NY: Artisan; 2000.

Kolata G. Live Long? Die Young? Answer Isn't Just in Genes. *New York Times*, August 31, 2006.

Kolata G. Far From 'Junk', DNA Dark Matter Plays Crucial Role. *New York Times*, September 5, 2012.

Kristof N. Professors, We Need You! *New York Times*, February 15, 2014.

Landau E. Born in male body, Jenny knew early that she was a girl. June 14, 2009. Available at www.cnn.com/2009/HEALTH/06/12/sex.change.gender.transition/. Accessed on March 14, 2015.

Latham J. The failure of the genome. *Guardian*, April 18, 2011.

Latham J. and Wilson A. The Great DNA Data Deficit: Are Genes for Disease a Mirage? Available at www.bioscienceresource.org/commentaries/article.php?id=46. Accessed on March 31, 2015.

Leininger B., Leininger A., and Gross K. *Soul Survivor - The Reincarnation of a World War II Fighter Pilot.* New York, NY: Grand Central Publishing; 2009. A remarkable investigation motivated by a parent trying to disprove the apparent transcendental connection.

Lewin R. Is Your Brain Really Necessary? *Science*, Vol. 210, December 12, 1980. Available at www.rifters.com/real/articles/Science_No-Brain.pdf. Accessed on March 31, 2015.

Lopez D. S., Jr. www.tricycle.com/special-section/scientific-buddha. Accessed on April 6, 2015.

Luhrmann T. M. Beyond the Brain. *The Wilson Quarterly*, Summer 2012:28-34.

Luhrmann T. M. Benefits of Church. *New York Times*, April 20, 2013.

Luhrmann T. M. Belief is the Least Part of Faith. *New York Times*, May 29, 2013.

Luhrmann T. M. C. S. Lewis, Evangelical Rock Star. *New York Times*, June 25, 2013.

Lusseyran J. *And There Was Light*. Novato, CA: New World Library; 2014.

MacFarquhar L. Last Call. *The New Yorker*, June 24, 2013. Available online at www.newyorker.com/magazine/2013/06/24/last-call-3. Accessed on May 8, 2015.

Mayr E. *What Evolution Is*. New York, NY: Basic Books; 2001.

Dr. McDougall at www.drmcdougall.com or Dr. Esselestyn at www.heartattackproof.com for examples. Accessed on March 14, 2015.

McGaugh J. L. and LePort A. Remembrance of All Things Past. *Scientific American,* February 2014.

Melina L. R. *Raising Adopted Children*. New York, NY: HarperCollins; 1998.

Meyer S. C. *Darwin's Doubt*. New York, NY: HarperCollins; 2013.

Mitchell K. A. www.wiringthebrain.com/2012/02/ive-got-your-missing-heritability-right.html Accessed on February 8, 2015.

Mitchell K. A. www.wiringthebrain.com/2012/07/genetics-of-stupidity.html Accessed on February 8, 2015.

Nature 1997. Cited in "Best is yet to come". *Nature* February 2011, 470:140. Available online at www.nature.com/nature/journal/v470/n7333/full/470140a.html Accessed on February 8, 2015.

Nestler E. J. Hidden Switches in the Mind. *Scientific American*, December 2011.

Nestler E. J. The Mind's Hidden Switches (podcast transcript) at www.scientificamerican.com/podcast/episode.cfm?id=the-minds-hidden-switches-11-11-22. Accessed on February 8, 2015.

Nisargadatta S. *I AM THAT*. Durham, NC: Acorn Press; 1973 (paperback printing 1999).

Nixon R. Adopted From Korea and in Search of Identity. *New York Times*, November 9, 2009.

Nurenburger J. I. and Bierut L. J. Seeking the Connections: Alcoholism and Our Genes, *Scientific American*, April 2007.

Oppenheimer M. and Lovett I. Zen Groups Distressed by Accusations Against Teacher. *New York Times*, February 11, 2013.

Overbye D. Elevating Science, Elevating Democracy. *New York Times*, January 27, 2009.

Overbye D. Astronomers Find Biggest Black Hole Yet. *New York Times*, December 5, 2011.

Padawer R. What's So Bad About a Boy Who Wants to Wear a Dress? *New York Times Magazine*, August 8, 2012.

Pasachoff J. M. and Pasachoff N. Physicists on Wall Street? *New York Times*, January 30, 2011.

Peat F. D. *Infinite Potential: The Life and Times of David Bohm.* Reading, MA: Helix Books: Addison-Wesley; 1997.

Petersen's Graduate Programs in Biological/Biomedical Sciences & Health-Related Medical Professions - 2014. Albany, NY: Petersen's Publishing; 2014.

Piekoff K. I Had My DNA Picture Taken, With Varying Results. *New York Times*, December 30, 2013.

Pinker S. *How the Mind Works.* New York, NY: W. W. Norton; 1997.

Pinker S. *Blank Slate: The Modern Denial of Human Nature.* New York, NY: Viking; 2002.

Pinker S. My Genome, My Self. *New York Times Magazine*, January 11, 2009.

Pinker S. *The Better Angels of Our Nature - Why Violence has Declined.* New York, NY; 2011.

Pollard K. S. What Makes Us Human. *Scientific American*, May 2009.

Quiroga R. Q., Fried I., and Koch C. Brain Cells for Grandmother. *Scientific American*, February 2013.

Radin D. *Entangled Minds.* New York, NY: Paraview Pocket Books; 2006.

Ramachandran V. S. and Blakeslee S. *Phantoms in the Brain.* New York, NY: HarperCollins; 1998.

Reilly R. Heart and Seoul. *Sports Illustrated*, February 20, 2006.

Ricard M. and Thuan T. X. *The Quantum and the Lotus: A Journey to the Frontiers Where Science and Buddhism Meet.* New York, NY: Broadway Books; 2004.

Ruggerio R. Phantoms of the Forest. *Wildlife Conservation*, October 2000.

Sacks O. Seeing God in the Third Millennium. *The Atlantic*, December 2012.

Schafer A. genetics.thetech.org/ask/ask166 Accessed on February 8, 2015.

Scharf C. The Benevolence of Black Holes. *Scientific American*, August 2012.

Segal N. L. *Indivisible by Two - Lives of Extraordinary Twins*. Cambridge, MA: Harvard University Press; 2005.

Sekida K. *Zen Training*. New York, NY: Weatherhill; 1985.

Shariff A. F. and Vohs K. D. the world without free will. *Scientific American*, June 2014.

Sheldrake R. *Science Set Free: 10 Paths to New Discovery*. New York, NY: Deepak Chopra Books; 2012.

Shulevitz J. Why Fathers Really Matter. *New York Times*, September 8, 2012.

Siebert G. The Animal Self. *New York Times Magazine*, January 22, 2006.

Smith P. K., Cowie H., and Blades M. *Understanding Children's Development, Third Edition*. Malden, MA: Blackwell Publishers Inc; 1998.

Solomon A. How Do You Raise a Prodigy. *New York Times Magazine*, October 31, 2012.

Solomon A. *Far From the Tree*. New York, NY: Scribner; 2012.

Sowell T. *Einstein Syndrome - Bright Children Who Talk Late*. New York, NY: Basic Books; 2001.

Sowell T. *Late Talking Children.* New York, NY: Basic Books; 1998.

Stevenson I. *Where Reincarnation and Biology Intersect.* Westport, CT: Praeger Publishers; 1997. A pretty dense, clinical-like read.

Strong J. S. *The Experience of Buddhism.* Belmont, CA: Thomson Wadsworth; 2008.

Tart C. T. *The End of Materialism.* Oakland, CA: New Harbinger Publications; 2009.

Tenneson M. Siblicide - Who Says You Have To Be Nice To Your Brother? *Wildlife Conservation,* September/October 2006. Tastefully no photos were included.

Tobias M. *World War III.* Santa Fe, NM: Bear & Company, Inc; 1994.

Treffert D. A. *Islands of Genius.* London, UK: Jessica Kingsley Publishers; 2010.

Treffert D. A. Accidental Genius. *Scientific American,* August 2014.

Thondup T. *Peaceful Death, Joyful Rebirth.* Boston, MA: Shambhala Publications; 2005.

Thuan T. X. english.trinhxuanthuan.fr/home/Books-published/buddhism-science/buddhism-science Accessed on February 8, 2015.

Tucker J. *Life Before Life - A Scientific Investigation of Children's Memories of Previous Lives.* New York, NY: St. Martin's Press; 2005. Contains a number of Western cases and is considerably more readable than his former colleague Stevenson's work.

Tucker J. *Return to Life - Extraordinary Cases of Children Who Remember Past Lives.* New York, NY: St. Martin's Press; 2015. Includes more Western cases.

Venter J. C. *Life at the Speed of Light: From the Double Helix to the Dawn of Digital Life.* New York, NY: Penguin Books; 2014.

Wade N. A Dissenting Voice as the Genome is Sifted to Fight Disease. *New York Times,* September 16, 2008.

Wade N. A Decade Later, Human Gene Map Yields Few New Cures. *New York Times,* June 12, 2010.

Wallace B. A. *Hidden Dimensions: The Unification of Physics and Consciousness.* New York, NY: Columbia University Press; 2010.

Wallace B. A. *Meditations of a Buddhist Skeptic.* New York, NY: Columbia University Press; 2012.

Web presentation. www.int.washington.edu/users/mjs5/ Simulation/Universe/. Accessed on April 4, 2015.

Yuste R. and Church G. M. The New Century of the Brain. *Scientific American,* March 2014.

Zimmer C. The Search for Intelligence. *Scientific American,* October 2008.

Zimmer C. Is Most of Our DNA Garbage? *New York Times Magazine,* March 8 , 2015.

Made in the USA
Lexington, KY
08 June 2016